D1551650

FORWARD

It's still true, nothing succeeds like success! With this book, I invite you to begin you journey to professional success. Psychologists say that superior intelligence may avail nothing along the path to success and happiness. Hard work is not the answer. Dedication and loyalty may be insufficient. Talent can remain idle and unknown. While you need not have a great intellect or great talent to be successful, you do need to master fundamental principles that brings success—and this book gives you the secrets.

Within you there is a resevoir of wisdom; a seed of truth waiting to be discovered. When you seek to live a more successful life, what matters most is not what you know, but the action steps you take to reach your goal. Most important of all for those who have many goals, is the fact that the qualities that lead to economic security are the same qualities that lead to a more meaningful life.

Is there a Law of Success? There is. Can we learn what it is? We can. This inspiring book is chock full of timely information and tips on how to improve the quality of your life. Drawing from 20 years experience, the author teaches simple, easy to follow strategies you can use to experience success in all areas of your life. With Henry Leo Bolduc as your personal guide, you will experience teachings that have touched his own life directly. *Your Creative Voice* will show you how to write more effectively, how to become a better communicator, and how to present successful workshops.

We owe Henry leo Bolduc a profound debt of gratitude for granting permission to distribute this special edition of *Your Creative Vocie* to members of the National Guild of Hypnotists, Inc.

Dwight F. Damon, DC
President/Executive Director
National Guild of Hypnotists Inc.
Merrimack, NH 03054

YOUR CREATIVE VOICE

Reaching and Teaching From Your Experience

Henry Leo Bolduc

ISBN Number 0-96 013 02-0-9

 Adventures Into Time Publishers
P.O. Box 88, Independence, VA 24348, USA

Manufactured in the United States of America

*To Advise
and to Imprint
the Spirit of Truth*

Contents

Acknowledgments

Writing a book is a birthing process. Of course I was a part of the conception, gestation, and arrival of this book. Many others also are responsible for its safe delivery into your hands.

The care and nurturing of such a promising baby was provided by these maternal godmothers: Linda Hutchins, Ruby Gillion, Rosemarie Deering, and Marjorie Reynolds, my Canadian friend and final editor.

Rocking, burping, bathing, and diapering (fine-tuning and typing!) were offered generously by: Peggy Becker, R. M. Gray, Pam Mellot, Charles L. Miller, Clara Roberts, Jennifer Page, and Susan Hufeisen.

Baby was made "picture perfect" by artists/illustrators Kathye Mendes, Jeffrey Winchester, Diane Coleman, Julia Fierman, and Sue Jones, who also designed the book's cover and placed the entire manuscript on computer disk.

Now that our baby is alive and smiling, I plan to trust it to the capable hands of its natural mother — my wife, Joan. Like any normal father, I assume that she will wake at odd hours to feed it, to change it, to rock it, and to love it!

— Henry Leo Bolduc

Artist: Kathye Mendes

Introduction

Many individuals are searching for a real purpose and value in life. Some people say, "If I knew my purpose in life, I would pursue it." *Your Creative Voice* welcomes you to embark on a wonderful journey — to discover value and meaning in your life. It welcomes you to the fullest life imaginable — to adventure and discovery. It welcomes you to the creation of miracles through a new way of communicating. All of those things could happen just by chance; however, you also should prepare yourself for exciting changes. *Your Creative Voice* will help you to discover your purpose or mission in life through a common sense approach — prudent actions based on practical knowledge and experiences. You will learn "people skills" and "life skills" to prepare for this transformation.

Imagine if every person, including YOU, began to share individual knowledge and experiences as teachers, leaders, visionaries, and healers. Imagine the inspirational climate for future generations as they prepare themselves — physically, mentally, spiritually — to grow as stewards of the earth. Whatever you live today is planted for future generations. Prepare the soil in which the seeds of miracles can germinate. Create an atmosphere in which miracles can thrive. Whatever you teach, write, or speak today will be harvested by humanity tomorrow.

It is easy to sit back without sharing your individuality. Both ancient and modern sources describe the fault, or sin, of omission as a person who **could have** done something to help others but chose not to do so. You have a right and a responsibility to be of help and service to humanity. *Your Creative Voice* helps you open new doors to inform others that you have a timely and important gift to share in a world on the brink of spiritual bankruptcy.

Your Creative Voice is intended for the rare and wise people who wish to express unique statements or visions for these changing times. Whether you realize it, **you** are already expressing your life in some way. You might ask yourself, "What have I devoted my life to?" The answer is to be found in whatever you are doing right now. What is it that already occupies your daily life? You reflect who you are in what you are doing, and you display that to others. This is how you are living out some purpose.

What is your talent? What do you love to do? What REALLY excites you? That is your gift or skill. Each person has something wonderful to share. The best way to share your gift is to start right now — speaking, writing, teaching, and living it! Start today. Do something constructive in any field that interests you. Although formal education is important, you do not need any special qualifications, degrees, or financial wealth to share what you have learned.

For instance, if you love nature, then go out into her very bosom. Tell others about her beauty, write about her majesty and wonder. If you love to love, then teach people to become better lovers. Give classes in the art and adventure of loving. When you search your own ideals and purposes, you'll discover what it is that you desire to share. You have the God-given right to share your research, insights, and discoveries.

When you do something that you enjoy, you will become more intuitive — attuned to the creative process — both consciously and unconsciously. You can succeed in learning to work at both levels. It is just a matter of doing it. In the **doing** comes accelerated learning in communication processes. *Your Creative Voice* goes beyond the basic skills of writing, speaking, and teaching by utilizing the unlimited potential of your subconscious mind. At the end of this book, there are guided session scripts to make positive programming tapes that will help you at the inner (subconscious) level. This is the level of creativity and genius. Here is your added edge — your true springboard for success. Note that this is an authentic and honest book — there are no grandiose schemes, no promises of effortless wealth, rather a unique combination of conscious learning and subconscious programming. You have the potential to be anything you wish to be. If you are willing to learn, you can make your dreams a reality.

We learn in two ways: (1) consciously through trial and error experiences and (2) unconsciously through intuition, prompting, and contemplation. By utilizing the three guided session scripts, presented in Chapter 9, this book affords the opportunity for you to increase the effectiveness of your communication skills and to feel comfortable in doing many things that you may fear doing.

I did not set out to be a writer and a teacher, but my desire to share experiences and research gave me the courage to begin. I had limited formal academic qualifications, and English was not my first language. I was afraid to write because my inaccurate syntax, grammar, and punctuation might bring criticism and could detract from my work. In addition, I was scared during my first few times in front of an audience. Now, I have grown to love speaking (especially when conducting workshops), teaching, and writing.

In facing those challenges, realizing that writers face possible humiliation, I empowered myself to become a writer, speaker, and teacher. In the process, I have tried to encourage others. Realistically, however, the goal includes careful planning, hard work, much research, and attention to minute details. Professional qualifications are important; get them if you can. Should such certification be unavailable (or should seem inappropriate for you), then take the self-help, self-taught route. The overall vision or ideal makes it all worthwhile.

You might be thinking that there can be real joy in attaining a significant goal. A major goal is more than the culmination of a grand-scale event; it involves a series of adventures and accomplishments along the way. Just as in school, you PASS one grade at a time, each step must be appreciated and celebrated. In my three decades of work in my chosen area, much of my joy has come through reaching such short-term goals. Your joys could be many if you learn to accept successive approximations as successes and regard setbacks as not having learned yet. Take all the time you wish in working toward what you want to achieve. Choose whatever route seems appropriate for you.

I am sharing a considerable amount of information in this book. I hope it will not overwhelm you or cause you to become disillusioned. Evaluate your skills and what you really like to do, then start the fine-tuning.

In all endeavors, whether writing, speaking, or

teaching, you make mistakes. You flounder upon stormy rough seas and sail in wrong directions from time to time; yet, through those mistakes can come the greatest learning. This is called **controlled floundering.** You might fail at first, but you will improve by actually navigating the rough waters. You are strengthened for future success. That is what you did as a child when learning to walk. Did you learn to walk or are you still crawling?

This book is not a step-by-step approach to success; rather, its purpose is to encourage you to aim toward your highest level of fulfillment and creativity.

Who will be your greatest ally? YOU will be. Self-help is real help. It is the best gift that you can give to yourself. You already have many more skills than you realize. Develop and strengthen some of them. Add related skills. You will discover truths that you had not recognized. You will awaken potentials, maximize abilities, and discover hidden talents. Most of all, you will build courage — the courage to live life fully and to make miracles happen! Welcome to *Your Creative Voice* — the next level in a natural progression of transformation and outreach.

Chapter One
Writing to Learn — Writing for Fun

If you keep a journal, correspond with a friend, or record your dreams, you already are doing informal writing. If you do not write, it will be fun for you to learn. Writing can be enjoyable, and you can grow through the process.

As you begin to write, you might choose to start with an easy, informal project and then progress to a more professional work. Some of you, eventually, could write a book or even books.

The progression from informal to formal writing is a simple process — it's called growth. In life, we grow in stages, step-by-step, sequentially, progressively, with periods of peak or accelerated learning. That's the way life works!

If you actually enjoy writing, you are already a step ahead in the adventure of life. Whenever you enjoy what you do, the doing is fun, and the accomplishments are greater. If you view life as a constant wonder with excitement in discovery and enjoy the process of growth, your progress will be faster and better.

Your first steps are the most important because they are the foundation for other steps to greater learning. Study this chapter carefully and **DO** the exercises. Merely reading will accomplish little for your progress, but studying the material and doing the projects will be of immense benefit. The exercises suggest ways for you either to start writing or to enhance your current efforts.

Writing can be an effective vehicle for discovering your true self. Through writing, you can gain valuable insights about your own beliefs and values. Such discoveries can be a source of healing for yourself as well as inspiration and encouragement for others. The real purpose of writing is to acknowledge your thoughts and experiences — to record them for future use, evaluation, and enjoyment! Write for yourself; write to share with others. It does not matter which comes first.

If being a writer is appealing to you, then have faith in yourself and in your ability to make those dreams come true. Ask yourself if there is something within you that longs to be said. Do you have thoughts, visions, or experiences that you would like to share with someone? If you are compelled to say something, say it on paper. You might be a writer in the making! You can walk the path toward the writer's world by taking a few simple steps. One of the easiest is the step into journal writing through which you can record meaningful stories and valuable information which, in time, you could share with others.

Journal Writing

Your personal experiences will be the main focus of your journal. Many people associate journal writing with keeping a diary. A **diary** is certainly one type of a journal in its most basic form, a day to day account of events in your life which you choose to record for future reference.

Journal writing is inexpensive; your favorite pen and some paper put you in the writer's seat; you could use a three-ring binder or, perhaps, a computer, if you wish to categorize your subject matter. Journal writing requires no special training or preparatory classes. You can start right now — today! Just put your thoughts, feelings, and memories on paper or disk.

Begin by posing a question to yourself. For instance, how would you describe your family, your friends, or your rivals? Do you live in the city, country, suburbs? Rural or residential? Do you have specific family traditions? If yes, do you still adhere to them? Why? If not, why did you change or eliminate them? Did you create traditions of your own? How? When? Why? You may think of other questions you would like to answer in reference to your family. Don't limit yourself to just sentences — draw pictures, diagrams, or doodles. Have fun with this! Much writing begins as thoughts captured on paper and filed for future use. Over time, they accumulate and can be compiled into an article or book.

Journaling was an important step in the life of a friend of mine. After moving away from her family, she became lonely and depressed. In time, she began to put her life experiences into perspective. She recorded memories and soon detected definite patterns in her experiences which explained a negative trait she had always held — low self-esteem. As she continued to write, it became easier for her to get in touch with her feelings and to take responsibility for them.

Another technique to stimulate your writing is to document your **stream of consciousness.** Begin by writing everything that comes into your mind regardless of whether it makes any sense. This "journal conversation" occurs as a direct response to the stimuli that you receive from your own mind. How do you start the ideas flowing? Use an emotion to stir up a memory.

Artist: Jeffrey Winchester

Go into your storehouse of personal life experiences, and call up the memory, details, and emotions of a well-known or half-forgotten event. Perhaps you can remember a moment of anguish when others seemed to have forgotten your very existence, maybe a time when you were far away from home and felt over-whelmed by all the new faces and places. You might still feel the loneliness, fear, and pain of that event. Or perhaps you remember a moment of great joy, freedom, independence, or awe.

Record your thoughts at random and simply let them flow. If you can think, you can write. Recapturing memories with an exercise of this type can dredge up a well of experiences, inspire dreams of the future, or simply give a moment for reflection upon your life. The important thing is to write. Write anything! Get started in the act of placing words on paper. That is how every great writer started! You don't have to edit your work at this point. Just get words on paper.

When an exercise produces uncomfortable feelings (some life memories might be unpleasant), try one of these: (A) Imagine yourself in a comfortable place. This could be an imaginary place or a real one that you can picture in your mind's eye. Describe why this place makes you feel secure, happy, peaceful, whatever feeling it might evoke. (B) Remember a pleasant dream which you recently experienced. Record it, and describe why you consider it pleasant. What do you mean by pleasant? Who was in the dream? Where did it take place? Did it seem life-like or more like a fairy tale? If you dream (and everyone dreams), you can write about your dreams.

Another writing technique is the **freeform style.** Freeform uses only one rule: write as though you were talking. Set things down just as they come to mind. Relax and look around. What do you see? Do you own something of value? Is it of monetary or sentimental value? Who gave it to you? Describe this person. Was it a man or woman? A family member? A friend? An acquaintance? Why do you think they chose this particular item? What was the occasion for the gift? The time of year? Where were you living at that time? Record this train of thought. Such thoughts do not require a particular connection or structure. Just let them flow freely. You are the only person who can record your stories and your life experiences. So get out of your own way! Don't limit yourself by perfecting spelling and grammar at this point, just let your words and thoughts flow onto the paper or screen.

To stimulate more ideas for this writing exercise, record a few words or sentences that remain indelible in your memory. Describe how those few words influenced your life's journey. Some material might lack definite meaning or emotion, that's okay. In reality, many events in life appear unimportant.

You might feel the urge to let the ideas flow onto the paper without shaping them into any particular form. Feelings and thoughts are spread over the course of an entire lifetime — twisted together like clothes in a washing machine. It takes time to sort them out and to put them in an orderly perspective, to create order out of chaos. Once you begin to organize your journal entries, ask yourself if you truly understand your thoughts, feelings, and emotions. How do they impact every aspect of your life? Be aware of attitudes and modes of thought that might give a clearer direction for your life. If your journal entries seem confusing, don't worry about it. Just accept that you are capable of releasing some of your thoughts on paper. With practice, the thoughts will work into coherent statements and, eventually, become meaningful as a whole. This step takes time, patience, and dedication.

Life has been likened to a giant puzzle. Through time, we place the various pieces into a complete and clear picture. For now, making the pieces of your puzzle into a big picture is **NOT** the goal. The goal, simply, is to **WRITE**! If you already do so, that is wonderful. If you do not, now is the time to start. Much of the continuing work in this book depends on this foundation.

Prose or poetry? What is your journaling style? The language of the mysterious and magical mind can be expressed in many ways. Work with whatever tools your subconscious provides. Follow your inner guidance. If you are musically inclined, you could write songs to express new understanding; or, maybe, poetry is an option for you.

A popular form of poetic expression is blank verse which consists of unrhymed lines containing a free-flowing, impressionistic, but coherent train of thought. Sentences may continue from line to line, rather than conclude at the end of each line. Even ordinary conversation, as spoken, can be written in blank verse. Prose, on the other hand, is structured by paragraphs rather than by lines and can be written just as it is spoken. It is the ordinary language we use in our daily conversations with family, friends, and co-workers. Prose is our living language and is most familiar to us. Usually, written materials are presented in this form, and this could be your style for journaling.

Recognizing and evaluating patterns in your journal might take some time; however, once you have done this work, you can begin to explore the inner depths of your true self. A friend of mine is a prolific dreamer; she awakens in the morning with vivid memories of her dreams and uses a journal to record them. Many times, her dreams are symbolic of challenges in her daily living. Every day, as she records her dreams, she also analyzes her life. The two coincide so readily that she keeps two columns in her journal; one side for dreams and the other side for real-life events. In this way, it is easy to note the patterns and to resolve conscious questions through the subconscious guidance of her dreams. Although you might not remember your dreams consciously, it still is possible to receive guidance from your subconscious mind. Sit quietly and reflect upon a problem or challenge that currently is affecting your life. Next, ask your subconscious mind for a solution to that problem or challenge. When you receive an answer, write it in your journal.

Your current situation in life might be a continuation of themes from the past. Sometimes, it is helpful to look for recurring patterns or themes. In an effort to focus on some of the patterns, respond in your journal to the following questions: Whom do I hold as a role-model, an example, or a pattern to follow? Why is this person significant to me?

Journaling can reveal thoughts upon which you wish to build. What standards determine your behavior? Do you live by them? What are your beliefs, morals, inner convictions, attitudes, emotions? What dominates your thoughts? Remember, your mind is a builder — a builder of ideals — the standards which guide your life's journey. Setting an ideal is like planning a trip. If you were traveling from Maine to Arizona, you would not just choose any highway at random and start driving aimlessly. Of course not! You would follow a prescribed route to reach your destination. Incredible as it might seem, most people travel the most important journey, the journey of their lives, without the assistance of a mapped route. The life journey should consist of a dynamic awareness of living life to its fullest potential. What luggage — thoughts, beliefs, attitudes — will you carry with you?

What is the destination or ideal toward which you travel? Journal writing can help you to discover your route through life.

Therapeutic Tirade

Letter writing can be therapeutic. Often, people have disagreements and misunderstandings. It is not uncommon to experience deep-seated anger, fear, resentment, intolerance, and general confusion. Perhaps you have experienced such unresolved emotions and have been left feeling that things have not been settled nor the last word spoken.

Do you allow the feelings to seethe inside? With a stroke of inspiration, you decide to write those feelings in a letter so you can have your say without being interrupted. In this deeply emotional state, you conjure up every heated word in your vocabulary. You pour them across the page as you unleash your anger, hurt, or disappointment. You finish the letter, stand up, stretch, and go about your daily affairs feeling more at peace for having unburdened yourself through the written word.

STOP! Don't mail this letter now! Instead, put it into your journal. This will be an exercise in discipline and will be one of the landmarks in your emotional journey. Should you decide that the letter must be mailed, wait at least five days before actually putting it into the mail! Those five days will allow the emotions to settle, and then, you can decide if you **really** want to send it.

Once the initial heat of your anger has passed, you may seek a more constructive way in which to resolve your difficulties. You might see the situation from a new point of view; you might gain new insight about your inner self — your true self. Perhaps you will see another piece of the "puzzle of yourself" and how this piece fits into your pattern of growth and maturity. This experience can benefit both you and others. The process of identifying, understanding, and transforming disruptive attitudes and emotions in a productive way is important in the resolution of inner conflict.

Stories to Tell

Storytelling is an ANCIENT process of teaching and helping others. Everyone has a story to tell. Others can learn and can understand through reading or listening to that story. In addition, it can elucidate the understanding of one's own story.

Are you thinking, "Story writing? I'm not an author. I can't write a story!" In fact, statistics reveal that 90 percent of all Americans think that they cannot write creatively. You will never know for sure unless you try! First of all, don't begin by thinking you must write a book. Think in more modest terms. Write about what you know. Let the story tell itself; just sit down and do it! Writing stories can be just as much fun as reading them, and, as well, can be a very educational experience.

Remember, the most important writing you do is that in which you are emotionally involved. **You** are the subject. This is **your** journey. Begin with your personal experiences in any area. After all, you were there. You know better than anyone else what happened. Recall your sensory data: heat, cold, sun, rain, sleet, or snow. Remember how some conversation went. You, alone, know exactly how you felt and what you were thinking as the event took place. Only you can convey the true essence of your point of view. Knowledge comes from within. How is that knowledge gained? It is gained through activities and occurrences experienced in life. Your Book of Life can be written only by you. Begin recording those experiences now. The path of self-realization begins with you. Here are some "story starters" to motivate you and to get you going:

"The greatest teacher I ever had was …"

"A funny thing happened to me on the way to …"

"I would like to create …"

"My forefathers came to this country from …"

"My most memorable moment was …"

"The worst day of my life was …"

Maybe you won't choose to let your family or friends read or evaluate your first, or even your second, attempt at story writing; however, the feedback from this step can be very beneficial in helping you to prepare to share your writing with others. You'll learn to discipline your thoughts. You also will learn correct grammar, research skills, and many other techniques. In addition, you will give pleasure or impart knowledge to those who read your story. You even could have a story published. Then you can call yourself an author!

By journal writing, you will gain wisdom and experience. The positive emotions of love, joy, compassion, appreciation, and insight could spill over into notes or letters to friends, loved ones, and acquaintances. This correspondence will be recognized for what it contains, and both you and they will benefit from the sharing. In many instances, however, letters are written long before the person has the concept of journal writing. The wonderful opportunity to learn and to grow together can begin with letter writing.

In the years ahead when you re-read your journals, you might marvel that you actually put those thoughts

on paper! Some aspects of yourself that you recognize
might amaze you. You might even find it difficult to
believe that you made some of those entries.

Keeping a Journal

- Helps you to discover goals, ideals, hopes, fears —
  just about everything there is to know about you.
- Teaches you to **listen** — and listening more closely
  inspires better writings.
- Teaches you to **observe** — and observation brings
  vision to your writings.
- Teaches you to **touch** life more deeply — and this
  depth brings more feeling into your writing.
- Helps with self-honesty and personal integrity.
- Is a safe outlet for hurt, rejection, or reaction. It is
  your communication with the **real** you.
- Clarifies thinking.
- Substantiates your thoughts and experiences.
  Later, you can reflect upon them and gain different
  perspectives, over time.
- Is an opportunity for reflection.
- Gives a feeling of accomplishment. Writing
  exercises your mind.
- Opens a door to self-discovery by accessing your
  subconscious mind.

Chapter Two
The Magic Journey — Creative Writing

"Should you care to write —

and only the saints know why you should —

you must have knowledge, art and magic.

The knowledge of the music of words

the art of being artless

and the magic of loving your readers"

— Kahlil Gibran

Developing Writing Skills: The Work

An informal method of learning the art of writing is the self-discipline of starting to put your ideas on paper or on computer disk. Later, books or courses might help in the fine-tuning (including grammatical aspects) of writing; but the impetus to begin and the will to see it through must come from you. Be your own teacher.

Years ago, the term "self taught" carried an unintentional negative connotation implying that a person could not afford a formal education or lacked enough intelligence to be admitted into a school. Now,

Artist: Julia Frieman

Kahlil Gibran

the meaning is entirely different. Being self-taught and
self-educated clearly exhibits a degree of dedication far
above and beyond the standards prevalent in our world.
Self taught is the original meaning of the word
education, meaning to draw out what is already within
a person; not simply to be incorporating the beliefs,

styles, or agenda of a formal teacher. A self-educated person is a self-starter, self-director, eager to learn, and finds a mentor at the right time.

The appropriate timing can open up entirely new perspectives by generating and enhancing original ideas. There is an old axiom that states, "She didn't know that it couldn't be done, so she went ahead and did it."

When writing, strive for honesty, originality, and the freedom to express yourself in unique ways. Write from your heart rather than from your head. Think of future generations as you write and fashion your work so that it will reflect timelessness for those who will read your material in the future.

Always be kind in your writing; if something is harmful or egotistical, erase it. If you write about problems, be sure to offer realistic solutions, not merely the illusion of a solution. Write with the richness of simplicity; short, powerful words have life and depth. Write with vitality and excitement, not hype or pomposity.

Always read your work aloud. Rework it and read it again. In reading and rewriting, you will hone the great gift of creativity. Creativity originates, refines and nurtures itself. Creativity is a process. It might be born of an inspiration, but it lives and grows through attention and cultivation.

The best writing, like the best of anything, should be simple, honest, and strong. Less is often more. You have a story to tell and experiences to share. Tell your story honestly; share it in as clear a manner as possible. Your story is unique and your perspectives are worthy of sharing with others.

If you write to make yourself sound important, you'll lose; self-importance is a trap. If you write to please others, you could fail the standards set by critics. But if you write to please yourself, to give of yourself, and to open yourself, THEN you will succeed. You will gain because you will have reached others and touched their lives, their hearts, and their minds.

When the Going Gets Tough

The field of writing is a fickle one! Many famous authors had received rejection notices from publishers for years; then their "big break" came and all of their formerly rejected material suddenly and eagerly was sought. Some writers compose a work at a young age and hold onto it — perfecting it over many years. Kahlil Gibran wrote the first version of *The Prophet* at age fifteen. He reworked and fine tuned it for more than twenty years before its publication. Success can, and does, come easily for some writers, but, for most, it takes time, patience, and dedication.

I also began writing at age fifteen by transcribing and typing transcripts of my tape-recorded sessions of past-life regression experiments. It would be fifteen more years before I would see excerpts from those transcripts published in my first book.

Keep all that you write because, in time, it might become more valuable. You can update and utilize the early writings.

Writing is hard work. It has not come easily for me nor has the publication of my writing been simple to secure. Often, I have thought of abandoning writing altogether. I also have wished that certain editors would be more kind or more generous in their attitudes toward my work; yet, in retrospect, this seeming hardship in my writing world has produced positive long-term results.

Perhaps if I had experienced an easy success, I would have become self-satisfied. I could have become smug and overly-contented. An early and effortless victory could have inflated my ego, and I might have become careless in my research.

An Excellent Adventure in Writing Articles

People occasionally ask the secret of my success in having published over 200 articles and commentaries in various newspapers, newsletters, magazines, and journals, along with some successful books, educational courses, and a regular column. There really is no secret to my success, but I can offer the following helpful hints to assist you on your way toward a happy publishing experience:

1. *Start with an easy project.* First, write "letters to the editor" for newspapers and magazines. Then, write articles for newsletters, magazines, and trade journals.

2. *Have something important, interesting, and helpful to say — even a personal experience to share that might encourage and inspire others.* The creative process is an important part of writing and, for a majority of people, it is the hardest. The knowledge and wisdom required to create an important article must come from your own interest and experience. You can touch the lives of many people by writing articles that will encourage, inspire, teach, or otherwise help others. Dare to share your thoughts and to speak your truths. You will be rewarded by the knowledge that you will have made a contribution.

3. *Write simply, clearly, and honestly.* Keep your writing simple, straight, and direct. Strive to provide your readers with valuable information that they can

use. You don't need erudite vocabulary or technical jargon. Even if you are writing for a professional journal, it is preferable to keep your writing as simple as possible. Young people interested in your field are eager to learn. Unless you are writing for a professional audience, aim your writing toward a seventh grade reading level.

Taking a course in creative writing can help. There are many books at the library which will provide guidance in grammar, syntax, style, and so forth. A good reference is a slim volume entitled *The Elements of Style* by William Strunk and E.B. White (published by The Macmillan Co.).

4. *Put your words on paper.* Once you have composed an article in your mind you are ready to commit it to paper. Handwritten manuscripts rarely are read by publishers, so it is imperative that you type your work.

If you plan to do any substantial amount of writing, it would be a good idea to invest in a word processor or computer. Word processors are now comparable in price to a good typewriter, are easier to use, and will make you more productive.

Some people are frightened by the thought of using a computer, but there is nothing magic or mysterious about them. Just think of their keyboard as your typewriter and the screen as your sheet of paper. As with any skill, you must learn how to use it. (After all, you didn't learn to print or to type without practice, did you?) Computers are becoming easier and easier to use and with a little effort and practice, anyone can master them.

All aspects of human experience are changing dramatically. The field of computers is certainly high on that list of change! In virtually every field, computers play a far greater role than just as tools for word-processing and accounting. As computers become more "user-friendly" and more compatible with other computers' language, the world will be speaking the same universal language of information. While computers are not a substitute for creativity or courage, they definitely can ease the mechanics of writing.

5. *Ask friends and neighbors to critique your articles.* Begin by composing and typing the first draft of your article. This draft should be double spaced with wide margins so that your reviewers will have room to write their comments and suggestions. Then, make several photocopies and ask friends, family, and co-workers for their help in editing and improving the article. Ask them to write any thoughts or changes directly on the copy in red ink.

Artist: Kathye Mendes

Let your heart do the writing.

Some people probably will not be of much help. They will just read your rough draft and give you a positive review. Others will be helpful with practical comments and suggestions. Your best help will come from the analytical people who, while appearing harsh in their criticism, provide valuable insight into the details of your work. Some people are blessed with a mastery of language and communication; others are not.

Put your ego aside and evaluate carefully all the suggestions and comments you receive. Thank everyone but use only what is helpful. No matter how good a writer you are, your work will benefit from another person's perspective. So, **always** get as much help as you can.

I developed this approach because English was not my first language. My syntax was off, and I truly needed help. In this process I have been assisted by numerous people, have made new friends, and have learned a great deal. Even THIS book that you are reading was edited and improved by friends.

If one or two people are especially helpful to you, be sure to do a favor for them in return or work out a mutually agreeable form of payment for their help.

6. Employ multiple submissions. Send typed articles to every publication that seems appropriate for the subject of your article. Now visualize your article as finished, polished, and ready for publication. It is crisp, insightful, brilliant, and easy to read. People will love it! How do you get it into print? Submit your article to every appropriate prospect.

Send editors only typed (or photocopies of typed) articles. Your introductory paragraphs are very important. If they are intriguing and well-written, the editor probably will read the remainder of your submission and will decide if and when it can be used in a specific publication.

Do not become discouraged if your article is rejected. Consider it a rite of passage. Even articles by well-known authors have been rejected at one time or another. Publications need articles for print in the same way that newspapers need news to report. So, in time, with patience and perseverance (prayers also help), you **will** succeed. So I repeat, make **lots** of submissions; your article might even be accepted by more than one publication.

Let's turn now to another matter; that of payment for your article. Let's assume that you have done well. You wrote a first draft and friends assisted in critiquing and in fine-tuning it so that it turned out to be a great article. An editor liked it and has decided to publish it. Now, how much will a publisher pay you? In some fields, you will be paid **very** well. Some magazines and journals pay generously. The sad news is that most self-help or inspirational publications pay very little, if anything, for articles. Most likely, in those fields, you won't receive any money at all for your work. Why bother? Because you will gain in more ways than you would expect.

First and most importantly, you will gain by giving the gift of your knowledge and experience to humanity. Secondly, people will acknowledge your name as an author. This recognition can be helpful if you have a full- or part-time career in a particular field because successful, published articles can substantiate and authenticate your professional status. Thirdly, if you enjoyed writing short articles, you can work your way up to longer articles or a book which is the equivalent of about 12 to 16 related articles bound together.

A new career in writing waits to be launched!

But First ...

Many professional writers send a *query letter* before they begin any article or paper. The query is a one or two-page letter addressed to an editor in which you outline your thoughts on a certain topic. You explain your ideas and tell how your article would be relevant and important to the readers of that publication.

If you already have written an article, you certainly will need a query letter to introduce both you and the article to the editor. Do not submit the article unless it is requested. Simply state in your letter its relevance to the publication's subscribers.

Should the editor like your proposal, you will be asked to submit your article. Even then there is no guarantee that it will be accepted for publication. If you **are** asked to submit your article for review, compose a cover letter in which you remind the editor of your previous correspondence. Thank him or her for expressing an interest in your work.

When you become more experienced at writing, the query letter will prove even more crucial. When you are ready to write your book, or to ask a publisher to review it, a query letter is a necessity. A query can prevent loss of time and disappointment, and it will help you to focus your attention and your skills into areas that sell.

Taking it On the Chin: How Criticism Can Help You!

An amazing bonus in life is that, when you learn more about yourself, you'll become a more discerning writer. Conversely, as you become a better writer, you'll learn much more about yourself in the process. This is the secret of learning. We learn as we grow and grow as we learn.

Do not be concerned if you are overly critical of yourself at times. This is just your way of encouraging yourself to excel. Challenge yourself, and you will accelerate growth; but don't be too hard — there is a risk of becoming cynical in the process.

Be alert if others are critical of you; use their criticism as a guideline to be sure that you are clear in your vision and straight in your purpose. Accept criticism gracefully, even thankfully, and you will grow even more. Should the criticism be accurate, then change and grow accordingly. If not, then what of it? Let it go!

Every great person, indeed, everyone at some time has undergone criticism. This is a fact of life. Think of any person who ever did anything outstanding, and you will find that person's antagonists and critics. Perhaps such adversaries, in some unexpected way, even HELPED those people to become great!

If you cannot handle criticism, or if you fall apart when confronted, then you had better curl up and hibernate. Life *is* a challenge. Pioneers have distances to travel. Researchers engage in work that is demanding. Writers have critics. Be prepared to incorporate this truth into your experience.

As you become a writer, develop a balanced attitude. Be bold but not foolhardy. Be wise, but not smug. Be kind, but not a pushover. Be happy, but not delirious. Make time for solitude, but do not be a recluse. Be dedicated to your work, but make time for treats and retreats. Be concerned that you live your life to the fullest.

Chapter Three
There's a Book in Your Head

After writing comes publishing. The purpose of this section is to encourage and to inspire you to get your material published.

Obviously, there are many techniques, pointers, and "trade secrets" in the publishing industry. You might prefer to find a publisher who will print your book or you actually could start where you are and do it yourself. Yes, you can write **and** publish your own book!

Some sources, such as book publishers, can help you learn the steps involved in bringing out a book. A second choice would be to go to your public library and read books on self-publishing. No matter which course you choose, **learning** is really in the **doing.**

A Family Matter

Although I freely admit that I love self-publishing, not everyone shares my enthusiasm. In fact, my wife Joan and I have had debates over this very issue. She gently reminded me that I could not afford to print so many materials and simply give them away. She felt that printing was an unnecessary expense, and frowned upon my proliferation of booklets and manuals. I appreciated her concern, but I believed that such materials were valuable additions to my workshops. I hoped that, through printed materials, my work and research would be made available to future generations.

Then something happened to change the focus of our debates. Joan had compiled a booklet which encourages parents to begin reading to a child at birth and to continue this practice throughout childhood. She received funding to print this booklet through the library literacy program which she coordinates. *Read to Me... I'm Yours* brought acclaim and appreciation from area communities and from educators at state adult education and literacy conferences. A little booklet can go a long way.

Copies of *Read to Me... I'm Yours* were distributed to new parents at all area hospitals, health departments, head start centers, and libraries. A few discount stores gave them free to customers holding babies.

Read to Me... I'm Yours was so successful that it went into a third printing. Then the literacy program received a grant to publish a new booklet for parents of pre-school children. Joan has been fortunate in having her creative projects funded by others. Her new booklet entitled, *Read to Me... I'll Read to You* was born.

Through the process of compiling and designing those booklets, Joan changed her attitude. Now she understands my commitment to publishing and the joy of giving such valuable material to others. Now SHE paces the delivery room at the local printers!

I hope that you will discover the great joy of taking blank paper and turning it into something both informative and beneficial to others. If you include artwork, you can enhance its beauty. You might be fortunate enough to receive funding and then it won't cost you ANYTHING to produce your materials.

Artist: Jeffrey Winchester

Now SHE paces the delivery room at our local printers.

Funding can come from unexpected and unusual sources. I have to pay for my printing, but I perceive the expense as an investment for the future.

How to Begin: Booklets Before Books

If you are a timid writer, it would be wise to start with small tasks before tackling a big project. Before writing a book, write a booklet or a manual. Before publishing a book, have a booklet printed. You will learn so much in the process, and you'll save money by avoiding costly mistakes later.

Here are some reasons for starting your publishing venture with a booklet:

1. A booklet is a new field wherein you expand your world and develop new skills.

2. A booklet is inexpensive to produce. Even photocopy shops can compile attractive booklets at a reasonable cost.

3. The cost of production can be less than one dollar while your booklet might sell for several dollars. Your profit will not be large for there are hidden costs such as time, artwork, etc. Your first attempt will show that there are greater possibilities ahead.

4. A booklet is an excellent way to test a new market or new materials. You soon will learn that some topics or titles sell better than others. Such marketing experience is valuable. You'll realize that what people SAY they want and what they actually PURCHASE could be very different.

My introduction to booklets was at the Providence Hypnosis Center where I began working in 1975 and, later, became the director. Customarily, the center gave a one-sheet set of instructions which reminded clients of the self-hypnosis procedure presented at their third and final session.

I recall thinking how uninspiring that one page looked and how I wanted to improve and to expand the material. At that time a photocopy cost ten cents. I took upgraded information to a local printer. The booklet emerged with a number of pages, a nice cover, and a much more professional appearance. Best of all, the cost of the finished product was only 22¢ for each booklet.

The extra 12¢ transformed the center's instructions from one page, which people soon discarded, to an attractive booklet that clients kept — and used— for self-hypnosis. In fact, many years later, I happened to see one of my clients at an antique show, and she told me that she, occasionally, takes the booklet from a drawer near her bed and uses the self-hypnosis techniques as a natural sleep aid.

During the two decades since my work at the Providence Hypnosis Center, I have produced numerous booklets. Booklets, in many cases, led to workshop manuals, which are basically larger and more expanded booklets. Some of those booklets and manuals led to books. The secret is taking small steps to a better product and a better future.

And Now ... a Book

Books are like gifts to present and future generations. There's a book in your head. **Writing** a book is likened to conceiving a child. **Publishing** the book is like birthing the child. **Promoting** the book is akin to nurturing and raising that child.

There IS a book inside of you that needs to come out. The only question is: Do you know what it will be about?

What Your Book Should Be

Your book should be fresh and engaging, offering either new material, or a fresh perspective on old truths. It can illustrate personal experiences from your own life. Write about your experiences and, especially, about what you learned from them. Show your readers how they can learn vicariously from **your** discoveries or mistakes. Most of all, it should be enjoyable to read. Write a book that is so helpful, so funny, or so exciting that people just have to tell their friends about it.

What Your Book Should Not Be

Since the world has enough complainers already, a "bitch-a-thon" is not a good idea. Don't waste your valuable time, or that of your readers in complaining and grumping. Use that time, instead, to offer realistic and innovative solutions to problems. Your book should NOT be what others have done; it cannot be a rerun of another's work.

Why You Should Write Your Book

A person becomes active in a specific area for a particular reason. In fact, most people do things for a number of reasons or fail to do things for certain reasons. What would be **your** reasons for writing or publishing a book?

A book is a valuable means of sharing your work and your thoughts with future generations. Books span the limits of time and place; they reach out to those yet unborn.

Books are the written record of humanity; they document important eras of history. The saga of human experience upon the earth is revealed in books, the highs and lows, the cycles of war and peace. Civilizations of which nothing has been written or for which no records are preserved are remembered only through legends. Entire civilizations have been forgotten for lack of recorded histories.

Books cost little and offer much. Your professional prestige will be enhanced when the subject of your book is related to your career. For example, in my field of hypnosis and past-life exploration, the books help to substantiate my research and they serve as outreach.

In the long run, outreach pays more than royalties. If you have clients, a book can increase the number of those seeking therapy or counseling sessions, or whatever it is that you offer.

To get media coverage, you will need to contact the local media and open a door to opportunity — they WILL respond. Media coverage will enhance your work. You can ask for an interview or a book review from local and regional newspapers. Contact local radio and television stations and any city magazine where such outlets are available.

A book often opens doors for you to speak to groups and organizations. Somehow, a book establishes the author in ways that nothing else can do. Producing a book IS a lot of work (as anyone who has ever attempted it realizes). Often, authors are treated with great respect. You might even be invited to "literary teas" if you can bear such socializing!

Local bookstores might sponsor you for an author's book signing. They will make money from the sales and are happy to get attention drawn to their shop. You could develop new friends and a "following" from such events.

When people read your book, they will want more information; this experience opens a natural way for them to come to your workshops or lectures. The long-term benefits to you and your public are of great value.

Seriously consider writing your book. A book is a profound accomplishment, and it might touch the lives of countless people everywhere. Most of all, it can reach into future generations and guide future discovery. Many people ALREADY have a book(s) inside — the secret is to get it out onto paper!

Getting Down to Business

There are, basically, three ways to write a book. One way is to work **slowly** and **carefully,** spacing the project over many weeks, months, or years. This method provides a carefully paced and specifically allotted time period. Regular worktimes could be scheduled or could occur at random.

The second method is total immersion. This system is like taking a vacation away from home and is an all-consuming — full time, every waking minute — kind of work. To accomplish the task, one actually could stay at home and intensively "do" the book. This seclusion might seem like being in a different world. Concentrated, active, and dedicated work often can produce a full book in a remarkably short period of time.

The third method is my favorite. Write when inspiration strikes! There are no rules other than grabbing the inspirations and thoughts and recording them on paper.

When Inspiration Strikes

Each person finds his or her best methods, time frame, and environment for writing.

My best method is scribbled notes; my best time frame is usually while driving long stretches of highway; and my best environment also is in the car — for inspirations! A rough copy comes first, of course, and then I work in my office for fine-tuning. I did not realize this process until recently when I stopped to evaluate how, when, and where I do my best writing.

Some writers set aside a certain time each day for their work. Some days they produce well and on others only a little. Sometimes, the material is great and sometimes it's destined for the trash. Other writers have no set work periods but are open to inspiration at the most unexpected times — often awakening in the middle of the night! (Spouses find this method frustrating to say the least, and I suspect that a few great writers live alone for that very reason).

As for myself, writing comes in its own time and in its own way. Often, material will come that does NOT concern the project on which I am currently working. In such cases, I will make notes and file them away for future composition. Whenever I actually go into that file, I am amazed to see what is there. Happily, most of it is applicable to a current project.

Again, the years have taught me that my very best inspirations come while driving. In the past, I would try to stop on the side of the road to jot down those flashes of insight or even actually attempt to hold a notepad and make notes. Both of those methods almost got me killed! Then I discovered a small and inexpensive invention that, literally saved, my life: a notepad on a plastic suction-cup holder that mounts on the windshield. By using this pad, I can jot notes safely while keeping my eyes constantly on the road. The little notepad holder costs only a few dollars and is one of the practical inventions of our time. If you receive inspirations for good material while driving, this item is indispensable.

The most important aspect of this "inspiration method" for creative writing is to appreciate what we are given. If we acknowledge what is given, whether from our own mind or from some higher guidance, and IF we utilize the material, more will be provided. Somehow, our mind tests us to see what we'll DO with inspirations. If we recognize them, but fail to use them, then little more comes. If, on the other hand, we appreciate each inspiration and **write it down** for later re-working, fine-tuning, and polishing, then, more will be given.

It's a bit like cooking for your friends. When you prepare a special meal, one or two diners might seem unimpressed but will thank you out of politeness. Other guests might be excited by the dishes (you've connected with their inner beings!) and compliment your excellent culinary abilities. Now, tell the truth: which of those friends do you invite again for dinner? Appreciation opens the channel to more good food and to further inspirations!

Now, here is some food for thought! Often while on the road, I will take my notes into a restaurant and rewrite them during lunch or while enjoying a snack. This captures the immediate moment and all the thoughts surrounding a concept while they are fresh in mind and the juices are flowing!

Sometimes, as all writers do upon re-evaluation, I find that some of my notes seem worthless. But other ideas will grow and thrive and evolve into entire articles or even books! Creativity is a learning and growing experience for me. Is it for you?

Do you get flashes of inspiration? Do you stop and acknowledge them? Do you appreciate and polish them? Do you prefer to write "on demand" by setting aside a block of time? How have you done your best writing? What is your favorite environment, your most productive time-frame?

Writing is an unprecedented opportunity for creativity. Write from the heart, and your work will have depth, passion, and meaning. Personal writing allows you to make discoveries about yourself and your world. You can express honest feelings and unabridged enthusiasm!

The more you write, the more you learn. The "thinking on paper" leads to true self-discovery and creativity!

Gathering Material — What Do You Know?

Sometimes, for a year or more, thoughts come and I write them down. Often, I do not even know, consciously, the purpose of the notes and sheets. I write, or type them, and keep them in a big folder entitled Material for a Book. Writing a book is like creating a big jigsaw puzzle. I begin by gathering up all of the pieces written (numerous sheets on related topics). Then I find an order in which to place them (putting the pieces together). At last, I have the full picture, what the book actually looks like. I am now ready to have an editor or two give the material continuity and eliminate unnecessary sections.

The secret of writing and publishing is to write about what you know, what you believe, and what you do. In other words, YOUR TRUTH. Write about your experiences. Write about what is powerful and meaningful within you. Forget theories; forget "head stuff" that sounds clever. Go with the HEART! This will be real and your writings will have a timeless quality and a simplicity that will touch the hearts of future generations.

Writing from the heart conveys your sense of mission, dedication, and purpose. You are close to your subject, for you live it each day!

My books, tapes, and videos are about my research and procedures. They have been developed for more than three decades. Even though it seems that I sell books and tapes, I am actually selling the fruits of decades of dedicated research and development. People are eager for that sort of material because it saves them years of individual work and testing. They are able to take what I have learned and shared, and then start building and growing from a much higher level of understanding.

People who report benefits from my research will, in turn, share those discoveries and experiences with others. Others, then, are able to design research projects based on previous research results. This is the process that builds a better world; this is the continuity of civilization and of life's natural progression and development.

You Already Might Have Written a Book and Don't Know it!

If you pursue any form of advanced education, you already have material for a book! Many excellent books are rewrites, in simpler language, of a master's thesis or a doctoral dissertation. If you were writing about any field and had a thesis to use, you would begin by simplifying the terminology.

Learn to use simple words with specific meanings. Readers appreciate clarity. I strive for straightforward language in my books. People tell me how much they appreciate the simplicity of concepts and the easy-to-understand language. Do the same in your work.

Remember "KISS": **K**eep **I**t **S**imple and **S**incere.

So, do you have an idea? Use what you already have and build from that. Another possibility is to utilize your regular writings in related ways. For example, for some years I have written a column for *The Journal of Hypnotism.* This is an excellent journal, mostly for professionals in my field. This column enables me to write timely topics on a regular basis. This effort helps to establish my reputation and standing.

Often, I am able to take some of those journal columns and combine them into larger works. In fact, two of my books contain sections that originally were columns. I rework the original, expand upon certain aspects, offer personal stories, polish it, and then a new book is in the works!

Dancing With the "Big Boys"

There was a time in the recent past when big city publishers controlled the book publishing industry. Their "best seller" lists told readers what to purchase thereby influencing people's choices in ways that were beneficial and advantageous to the publishers. That practice is changing, and it's about time!

Big city publishers primarily bought manuscripts from Literary Agents and, often, only those people connected with them were able to get books into print. It was difficult to get a book published if you did not have an agent.

Now, people have found new ways to publish. Manuscripts that were refused or rejected are now highly successful books because people took charge of their own work and material! This "self publishing" resulted in many best-sellers. The big publishers continue to profit from the self-publishing field. They buy books that are selling well. They purchase the rights to published books that have a "track record" of excellent sales. YOU can take your book and have it published. Then, if you invest the time and effort to promote it, the "big boys" may come to you and ask to dance. Then, you can really **celebrate** a major life accomplishment.

Literary Agent

If you desire a more traditional route to publishing, you can find a Literary Agent. An Agent can help you in many stages of writing — especially in finding a publisher for your book. Of course, you will have to pay a commission, but it is well-earned.

Paranoia in Publishing

Some people are fearful that unscrupulous publishers will steal their work. They fear that they will lose their money and that credit which should be given to them will go to others. It is true that such things might happen, but it's rare.

Paranoia is the recessive gene in a writer's DNA makeup. A healthy dose of "reality therapy" is the antidote. As a safeguard, you can photocopy your manuscript — even your rough drafts — and date them. You also could copyright your materials. A little security is wise; we lock our homes when we go on vacation, but exaggerated fear can be both foolish and inhibiting. Instead, strive to be the author of material that is important and valuable to mankind or write for the enjoyment of writing. This main goal should be your focus of attention. The rest will take care of itself.

Fear of criticism is yet another aspect of publishing paranoia. A well-known and highly respected publisher in my field, Richard Sutphen, tells of a woman who submitted her manuscript to him for publication. He liked the material and wrote to tell her that he would publish it — with only a few minor corrections. She wrote back, quite irate, and stated that her manuscript was "channeled directly from God" and that she would not give permission to change one word of it.

Patiently, Richard wrote her and explained that until God learned to become a better speller, the book would not be published.

The point here is that every author MUST be willing and eager to accept constructive evaluations from knowledgeable sources. It is always better to improve the quality of one's work thereby greatly increasing the chances of its seeing actual publication. A writer who plans to "go the distance" must shed paranoia.

Another possibility is to give FREELY of your materials to all humanity. No one can steal what is freely given! No one can steal the sunlight or the air; they are there, free to all. I give freely of my research, my guided scripts and my discoveries. People appreciate them and utilize my work. I consider it a great honor that they appreciate the work.

Why You Should Self-Publish

By far, the most important reason for self-publishing a book is that you will have full determination concerning its content. You have ALL rights to its income, and you have full control over future editions and any foreign rights. Those aspects might not seem so important to you at the moment but, with time, you will realize the vast significance of such value.

Please do not take my word as an absolute authority in this matter; instead, ask other published authors. If you are a big name and an easily-recognized personality, perhaps you will be treated well because the publisher knows that you will tell others about the treatment you received. Famous writers will tell you that even at the upper levels of fame there is often real and justified dissatisfaction.

When YOU choose to publish for yourself, you'll probably have an excellent relationship with your publisher. (I sure hope so!) You can work together; in essence, your right hand **knows** what your left hand is doing. You will be fair and straight in dealing with yourself. You will receive the money that you earned. You might not reach the broad audience of the big publishers, but you will reach those people who will benefit from your work.

Individuals who publish their own works and other "small presses" have many advantages over the conglomerate publisher. Small presses are free of the politics involved in big-time publishing and decisions are based on matters other than just dollars. Big conglomerates are, primarily, **businesses** and, as such, have to show large profits.

Smaller presses, by contrast, are willing to venture into new areas to support alternative views and to stand for truths even when those truths are not popular. What most people don't realize is that almost everything we hold as accepted truth today was once considered revolutionary or even impossible.

Look, for instance, at the birth of a nation — The United States of America. The idea of colonies breaking away from England was considered treason. Look at all of the accepted principles of science. Most were outlandish and heretical in their time. Look at the discoveries in healing, in education, in just about everything! Even if your book is AHEAD of its time, it is still worth publishing. Can you understand the importance of leading-edge research, discovery, and the publication of such materials?

But How Much Does it Cost?

Anybody can write a book for very little money, but it does demand time and dedication. Book publishing, on the other hand, requires some capital — either the publisher has to invest money for printing and promotion, or the author, if self-publishing, has to fulfill that task.

Usually, an author and a publisher hope to make money in their joint venture; yet, sadly, this is not always the case. Some books fail to make a profit; some even lose money. That is a fact of life. Other books do well, and some do exceptionally well. That also is a fact of life.

If your sole motivation to write or to publish is to make money, you might wish to consider a "safe" field such as romance or mystery novels. If your motivation is to help humanity, to bring in new knowledge, or to teach new techniques, then the profit margin is likely to be of less concern. Usually, all serious effort is, some-how, rewarded; but not necessarily by a quick income. Be willing to share what you have, and, in time, you will receive the benefits.

You may say, "Well, why do it if it might not make money?" The obvious answer is that we all do many things that cost us money, but we WANT to do them anyway. You are **entitled** to write and to publish your work. If you make money in the process, that is good. If not, it is still good that you fulfilled your mission.

All striving, with accompanying learning, is valuable. Your book is like a gift that you give to humanity and copies that don't sell can be given — literally! — as holiday gifts to family, friends, and colleagues. It could be one of the most valuable gifts they ever receive.

From Conception to Birth

My hope is to inspire you to write your book. Then you can find a publisher or you can self-publish. The entire process can take months or even years. Many good books, individuals, and organizations can help you (see the List of Resources at the end of this book). Your local library has books to help you with the **process** of self-publishing as well as books with lists of potential publishers. Your local library also can access virtually any book through inter-library loan.

Now envision your book in print. It's already accomplished. Hold that thought. Cherish that feeling of accomplishment. Use the self-hypnosis scripts in chapter nine to make this goal a reality. Use your MIND to build your best possible future. Regularly using self-hypnosis tapes will connect your creative potential to practical implementation — linking concepts to actual results. Conception gestates to birth.

In your constructive imagination, progress ahead in time to the time when the book is written and even published. The "baby" is born!

The Big Day

Once your book is published, you will receive an advance copy. This is a big day (for any author), maybe one of the most important days in your life.

Later, when cases of your books begin to arrive, you will have plenty of copies to give to friends and family. Be sure to send complimentary copies to those people who were instrumental in its gestation. The book's "helpers" are its godparents and they will recommend it to their friends and acquaintances. Some of your helpers (godparents) might think of this baby as theirs also, and they will work to nurture and to promote it.

Give complimentary copies to selected individuals whom you feel could be instrumental to the book's success. Write to the Book Review Editors of magazines to which you subscribe or to the newsletters of organizations of which you are a member. If you are aware of a publisher who handles books such as yours, send him or her a sample copy and a letter proposing the possible sale of rights to future editions.

Pray for guidance in this matter for you may be given insights concerning those to whom you wish to send a copy. Sometimes the most unusual inspiration later proves to be the KEY person involved in the book's long-term success. Trust strong intuitions and act upon that guidance. Seldom will a book promote itself. YOU must take an active role in insuring its survival and success.

When the Baby Arrives!

It is correctly said that publishing a book is like having a baby. The big day eventually arrives — the baby is born and delivered by a trucking company, not the stork!

Now I must share with you something very personal... and holy. How do you greet your new baby? I have asked some authors and most admit to an overwhelming desire to reach out and hug the baby. This is not some weird fertility rite, but an honest expression born over months of nurturing and gestation.

Even famous authors do it — in the same way that new parents hug their offspring. A few have even admitted to kissing the baby secretly! Hugging the new book is as acceptable as hugging your child. It's okay! You may do it with reverence and with enthusiasm. Celebrate a new birth.

My wife and I feel that books and babies are the true treasures of each age. Books are encapsulated wisdom. They contain the endless wisdom of the ages. It is through books that wisdom is channeled from one age into another. They connect the ancients to the present and will be the bridge to future time.

How to Get Your Book Into
Almost Every Country in the World

Your book can be of value and importance to people everywhere. It could help to change the lives of some individuals in ways more profound and wonderful than you realize. But how will people in distant places get the chance to read it?

There IS a tangible and practical answer: libraries!

If books are the true wealth, the sacred objects of an age, then libraries are the temples that house them. Libraries protect, display, and provide access to the great books for present and future generations. Libraries can be a type of "doorway" to the past and to the future. Do you want to look into the past? Libraries contain a wealth of knowledge on past people, events, civilizations, etc.! Do you want to send something into the future? Write a book. Two hundred years from now someone could go to a library and check it out! Libraries and the treasures they contain are our greatest gifts to the future.

Libraries ensure that the timeless river of knowledge flows from the past, through the present, and on toward the future. This continuity of knowledge is an integral link in human evolution and advancement. Libraries, whether public or private, serve humanity in real and vital ways, preserving the record of humanity's journey. Libraries exist in every large city and certainly in every country of the world. They exist to receive your book, too!

If you would like your book to be read by an international audience, the following is a proven plan to make it happen. I can assure you that it works, for I have used it. The cost is minimal and the **outreach** is vast!

First, go to your library and ask for the reference that contains listings of libraries around the world. If your local library is too small and unable to purchase a copy of this volume, it can be obtained for you by inter-library loan. Thousands of libraries are listed in this book. Some lists are arranged by country, others by topic (such as law libraries), and all library addresses are given.

Now, with list in hand, you have two opportunities for outreach. First, compose and then photocopy a letter which briefly describes your book and explains its importance. You could offer a special library discount and include an order form for purchasing a copy. Then, send copies of your letter to selected libraries and anticipate filling the orders as they arrive.

A second option (and the method I use) is to send a complimentary copy of the book to as many libraries as you choose. Most countries have a national library in their capital city. A copy sent to every major nation is a very good start. If you can afford it, send copies to all prominent cities within the countries of your choice. (Currently, there are approximately 260 countries in the world.)

Obviously, it would be much more rewarding, financially, to sell your copies rather than to donate them. But generosity has its advantages. Most libraries will respond with a "thank you" letter. The very nicest letters that I have received have come from Israel, South Africa, and Australia.

Here are a few of the tangible advantages of mailing your book, at your own expense, worldwide:

1. You will present your book and thereby your ideas to countless people around the world, people whom you might never reach otherwise.

2. You can look forward to receiving letters from readers, and possibly initiating meaningful correspondences.

3. The entire cost of this project may be deducted from taxes as advertising and promotion or as other business expenses. This deduction will include the cost of the books, the postage, etc. (For up-to-date and accurate tax information, be sure to check with your accountant.)

4. In every foreign country in the world there is an English-speaking community; and those people, more than anyone, appreciate access to new books and materials in English.

5. The very best part of this proven plan is the fantastic deal offered by your local Post Office! Books

can be mailed at an exceptionally low rate which greatly reduces your overhead and enables you to send your books around the world. Above all, when marketing your book, the greatest reward might not be tangible but spiritual. By sharing your written thoughts, you will have done a great service for the betterment of humanity — and for rendering that service there is no price tag.

Remember

Many people have likened writing a book to earning a Ph.D. degree. There is truth in that comparison. A book takes me one to five years to compile and then even more time to fully develop. When you write and publish YOUR book, you will appreciate this similarity. Learning is a life-long endeavour.

Like a degree, a book can lend stature to your work and enhance your income. People have become wealthy and famous through writing, publishing, and selling books. Successful marketing tactics are explained more fully in chapter six.

Keep a Record of Your Published Work

Keeping copies of your submissions, published articles, and other printed materials will be of long-term benefit. It will serve you in both practical and aesthetic ways. It's easy to do; you simply purchase an inexpensive 3-ring binder and top-loading polypropylene sheet protectors. Buy those which come with 3 holes punched so that they will fit into your binder. They will protect important documents. The advantage of this method is that you will have easy access to your materials because they will be organized in one place. This is more important than you might think, for as the years go by, it is easy to misplace various items. The binder keeps your writing safe and handy. If, for example, you should wish to update a particular article, you can locate the original in seconds and have it ready to work on.

Better yet, become computer literate. Then, keep all of your writings organized by category on your hard drive. Be sure to make back-up copies of your files!

Please learn from my mistakes! For many years, I failed to utilize this simple method, and I paid a dear price, often wasting many valuable hours in trying to find an old article or document. This can be very frustrating, resulting in valuable materials forever lost.

For the past few years, I have kept a binder (along with one involving yearly finances and another for upcoming workshops), and this system works well for me. Use this helpful hint as a guideline, and design your own record-keeping system.

As your articles are published, clip them out or make photocopies and place them into your binder. Constantly add to your collection of published work. Save whatever is valuable to you even if you don't perceive the importance of keeping a copy. In time, you'll be pleased that you did.

The aesthetic reason for organizing your work is that you'll see at a glance just how much you have accomplished during each year. At first, your progress might seem slow as you move into exciting new areas; but soon you'll have a **bulging** binder or many disks. You'll be amazed at how much creative work you have produced each year!

The binder or disk containing your published articles and printed materials (workshop flyers, workshop manuals, mail notices, lists of sale items, etc.) will help you through the hard times of discouragement. Everyone experiences discouragement and disappointment. Be grateful if your work is deemed worthy of criticism. Science assures us that for every action, there is a reaction. Any reaction keeps your work in the eyes of the public. Sometimes, you WILL be congratulated. That's life. Your binder or disks will give you something tangible to hold in difficult times, and it will give you something which is **fun** to appreciate in the pleasant times!

Support — Criticism

Some things seem obvious, but they are, nonetheless, of great importance and need to be discussed. In your work, you will have fine supportive people, and some of them will be harsh critics. This is inevitable. How you deal with this contradiction is vitally important.

Take time with those people who help and support you. Give them your friendship and support. Build on what is there and what is good; this can blossom and grow fruitfully. Be kind to your critics. They are simply objective, not intentionally harsh. It is possible for a supporter to be a critic — one who provides valuable constructive criticism. Be patient, be polite, and detach from it all. Bless your critics, they could become your future supporters.

A Publishing Success Formula

    A. Author a Great Book
+ B. Believe in it
+ C. Contribute to its growth
+ D. Develop marketing strategies
+ E. Educate others with interesting articles
+ F. Find a publisher or self-publish
+ G. Generate publicity and sales
= H. Happily enjoy its success

Chapter Four
Speaking — Challenge Your Thinking

Speaking

In the first three chapters, we explored how informal writing can grow to more polished works such as a booklet, an article for a magazine, or even a book. The two major forms of communication are the written word and the spoken word. Some people are more comfortable in one mode than the other, but you can develop skills in both types.

The natural sequence is speaking before writing. A child learns to speak long before he or she learns to write. Many professional speakers learn to present first and — if they write — write a book later.

Ideally, you will learn to develop your skills in both areas of communication. Perhaps the best plan is to improve your learning and teaching skills simultaneously. In subsequent chapters, we will explore how to take the best of your written materials and add your speaking skills to design classes and workshops. Sound a bit hard at present? Don't worry, the process evolves naturally through the doing.

Public speaking is a career as ancient as time. For me, the most rewarding experience is being able to speak about my true passion, my true beliefs, and to get paid for it! Although a career in public speaking stays the same, the audience is changing constantly. People are tiring of television programs which, many times, seem to be insulting their intelligence and limiting their choices. They are looking for positive alternatives rather than the gloom and doom of the news or fear-based "information" they are receiving. An appealing alternative, for many, is listening to a live person who gives them something to think about while providing a positive, encouraging, and uplifting experience.

The intelligent audience wants to hear someone who believes in and is knowledgeable about the topic being presented — someone who permits inner beliefs to show through. When you begin speaking, be sure that you pick a topic which illustrates what you really **do** know and care about. Finding your niche can be difficult if you are looking outside your own true interests. It is through **exploring** your interests that true passion can develop in your work.

If it has been some time since you allowed your true concerns to speak to you, you might need help to reconnect with your inner voice. Browsing through your local library or museum can cultivate new ideas or awaken old ones. Then, by speaking in public, you are sharing the essence of what is important to you with your audience. You teach them to reach higher levels just by your own example.

It is realistic to recognize that your topic of presentation will not be of interest to everyone. Just as you do not care to listen to everyone, not everyone will enjoy listening to you. There are, however, people out there just waiting for **you** to come along. Trust that you will find them and then proceed with your plans! Many different teachers and speakers are needed to reach everyone. Perhaps you feel that what you have to say is similar to the next speaker's material. Keep in mind that the way in which you present your subject, the words that you use, and the passion that you put into your topic along with your unique understanding and communication of it, comprise your winning formula.

Rehearsal

Practice giving informal talks or rehearsing in front of small groups of friends. Ask them to analyze your performance honestly. Be sincere about wanting honest feedback. Ask for constructive criticism and be grateful for the help. Giving your talk in front of a mirror, or better, in front of a video camera, also will prove worthwhile; however, there can be no feedback except your own analysis.

Your actual words are only a fraction of the overall performance. Practice pronouncing your words with inflection and expression. Put an emphasis on those words and sentences that best make your point. If you want to keep your audience's attention, your voice must not become a monotone. Notice your eye movements. Making eye contact with individuals is **very** important. Looking above the audience is noticeable! Let them know that you've noticed **them**! Express yourself with hand gestures as well as your body posture. By allowing animation in your presentation, you will express your meaning more boldly and you will "connect" with your audience.

People will respond if given the opportunity to participate. Ask for questions and comments from the audience. You could get feedback by a show of hands. Remember that each audience is filled with unique individuals. When you gather the special aspects of each into a whole, you cultivate group dynamics. Let each person's individuality help your presentation flow into the area that is best for that person. Whatever is perfect for your audience is perfect for you.

Most audiences will like to hear your personal experiences but be careful not to overdo it! Remember each person is there for personal reasons. When you tune-in to what is happening with them, how your words are opening up new doorways and new possibilities, then you've got it! Let that be **your** main focus. Have fun and allow yourself to be flexible with your outline.

Artist: Diane Coleman

Practice giving informal talks to small groups of friends.

It is important to have your notes organized, but allow the creative process and interaction with the audience to take place naturally. Don't appear too rigid or formal, because it will take away from your enthusiasm. When the audience realizes that you are willing to diverge from your planned presentation to allow them expression, a stronger bond is created.

Stage Fright

I don't know anyone who has not experienced stage fright in some way — be it the upside-down butterflies colliding in the stomach or that nauseous feeling telling you not to open your mouth! Practice might help to alleviate anxiety, and you can use friends as a "pretend" audience, but I have found it harder to speak to friends in such a situation than to speak to a real audience.

You might be surprised to discover that top rock stars speak of "stage fright" even after years of performing. One secret of their success is that they didn't let this stop them. They pushed through it realizing that the audience was counting on them just as your audience is counting on you.

Each group will be unique and will help to keep you focused and at your best. Adapting to different groups allows your job as a speaker to evolve and to become more challenging. You would become bored if the same questions and reactions surfaced each time. Being receptive to diverse questions will encourage you to learn and to grow in your area of expertise — one more reason why this profession is so exhilarating.

There is no actual way to "make" you speak publicly if you refuse to do so. BUT, once you begin, the excitement of sharing and teaching could become something you love. Analytically, speaking or talking to **one** person is the beginning of public speaking. From that point, you can speak to a couple of people, and then to a few more. Soon, you will be able to speak to a small group, then to a bigger group. Logically it works that way incrementally. Most people do not learn from logic alone — experience is a far better teacher.

Without question, most people fear standing in front of an audience. Why? Because it is a **new** experience, that's all. If you did it every day or every week, you would become accustomed to the sensation. I love it, so I assume that everyone else will also. Speaking is one of the most exciting ways in which to share knowledge and experience with others.

When a person first stands to speak, he or she sometimes feels a certain movement in the solar plexus area. This sensation is a natural body function indicating the secretion of adrenalin. ANYTIME in life when one is faced with new experiences or new situations, one might get a boost of adrenalin; it's natural and it's free! It's a gift from within! Facing your audience is the cause of your excitement and it stimulates what you are feeling. Identifying the actual cause of nervousness is enough for most people to appreciate what is happening and then go on with the program.

Overcoming Fear

There is a method for guaranteed success in overcoming the fear of speaking. I did it, and it works! It's termed self-hypnosis.

Through the course of life, I've learned to improve my public speaking. I experimented. I tried some things, and they bombed. I tried other things, and they were a success. Most of all, the preparation that I did in my own mind was the most valuable. Those little investments in self-help paid off with great dividends.

Take all the classes or courses that you wish. Read books, listen to tapes, or watch videos about public speaking. Use all the resources available. And, yet, remember you will accomplish far more in your work with your own **subconscious mind** — through self-hypnosis, positive programming, and creative visualization. It is something that **you** do, and the success is all yours. Positive programming helps you to enhance your present resources and talents, and it assists in developing **new** skills and abilities.

Chapter nine has three scripts for you to read into your cassette recorder to make your own self-help tapes. The purpose of the tapes is to train the mind at the highest and most profound level.

As You Teach, So Do You Learn

Your audience is open and ready to learn and to teach. Be a good teacher and let others find their answers within themselves. Let them understand that you are presenting **your** truth. If they do not agree with it, fine. Your goal is to help them to find their **own** truth. By listening to yours, they can awaken an awareness of their own truth. Discourage attempts by your audience to place you on a pedestal. This is an uncomfortable place to be. Being admired is okay but don't let it go further than that for your own good and that of others. If you are asked questions for which you don't have an answer, don't be afraid to say, you don't know the answer. Collect the addresses of those members of your audience who asked unresolved questions and contact them when you find the answers. This is one way you can learn from your audience.

Laughter Bonds

You speak to people every day about your beliefs and opinions. Speaking to an audience is exactly the same. You are telling a group of friends, some of whom you simply haven't met yet, how you feel and what you have learned. No pressure. An audience can be a group of friends that will have just as much fun laughing with you as you do laughing at yourself if you forget where you are in your presentation and need to look at your notes. In fact, such an incident lets them know that you are human, too, and even vulnerable. Humor, especially when it involves one's own goofs, is a key to being a good speaker. When a group of people laugh together, the room suddenly becomes harmonious, and everyone is more at ease. This is a wonderful blessing for any presentation. That is why many good speakers begin with a relevant humorous story or joke — to break the ice and get the attention of the audience.

Should I Be Paid?

If your topic of discussion is spiritually oriented, some traditionalists feel that you should be donating your time for the good of humanity, not receiving a paycheck. My response to this attitude has always been the same: "If you talk to my children and explain how you feel, and they would be happy to stop eating meals, I'd be happy to do this for free." Sometimes they get the point; sometimes they don't. But actually, while here on planet Earth, we play the games of planet Earth. Money is one of those games. Does your audience expect a doctor not to charge for services but to see patients for free? There are some people who are financially independent and can donate their time; however, most of us need money.

Others believe that when something is given without an even exchange it has no value. Many times when information is given without cost, it does not seem to be as respected. When someone pays me, he or she listens more carefully and is more apt to respond to my suggestions. Make it clear that if you were not doing this, you would be doing something else to make a living. It is your **time, knowledge, and experience** for which they are paying. As you continue to grow in this business, and your personal time is not as plentiful as it used to be, your time becomes even more valuable.

Nonetheless, in the early stages of your speaking career, gratefully accept **every** opportunity to speak even for free. You'll learn to refine your presentation, and you can tell audiences that you are available to speak at other events.

Secret of Financial Success: Create Your Own Job

What happens if you continually complain that you do not like your job? BINGO! You get laid off, fired, etc. Such a reaction forces you to look at what you **want** to do. Staying with your job because you think you won't find another is not a good enough reason. When you believe that there is no work for you that you can enjoy, you create a negative, self-filling prophecy.

Begin a business for yourself that you can enjoy. Take a step in creating a new and positive world for yourself.

One way to succeed in this world is to find a field or endeavor which seems right for you. Evaluate what you really like to do — then find a way to make it pay.

Your library has books about self-employment. Read those that look promising to you. Self-employment offers unlimited potential for vast success. There are certain requirements, however. You must be self-motivated and willing to work long hours, and you must work with diligence. Some careers are carefully researched and specifically chosen. Some come about in the most unexpected manner. My writing and speaking careers arrived without my realizing it!

About twenty years ago, when I worked at the Providence Hypnosis Center in Rhode Island, our therapies targeted cigarette cessation and weight control. Clients came on an appointment basis, and we did not over-book so that there were no long waits. Occasionally, a client failed to come for the appointment (usually smoking), and I would have that extra time while waiting for the next appointment. At those times, I was restless and had little to do.

Our secretary/receptionist noticed my restlessness (I probably drove her crazy by pacing back and forth!) and suggested that I do some writing. I already had produced a nice little self-hypnosis booklet for our clients, and she liked it. She even suggested that I write a book about my years of research and experience with hypnosis and past-life exploration; consequently, I started writing and I have never stopped! Little did I know how many books would follow the first, entitled *Hypnosis and Reincarnation* published in 1977, now out of print.

My speaking career also began unexpectedly. A client came in for therapy and did so well that she told her women's organization about our center. Someone from the organization phoned and asked if I would speak to the group, even offering to pay me. I agreed without asking any questions. I had spoken to small, informal groups, and I enjoyed speaking. This was another good opportunity to speak, or so I thought!

When the contract arrived, it stated that there would be MORE THAN 100 women present! Oh no! Professionally maybe I should not admit this, but I was frightened by that number. I asked other therapists at the center if they wanted to speak to the group. No takers! They knew better. I declined the engagement and returned the contract unsigned. I learned a valuable lesson in humility.

This was a reluctant beginning to a speaking career, but now I am extremely pleased if a group consists of **more** than 100 people. Fortunately, other speaking engagements were offered, and I accepted them all. Nurses from a local hospital visited the center, and their contact led to opportunities to speak at the hospital. Local schools, libraries, and two universities invited me to present programs and classes.

Most of my speaking engagements paid something if only travel costs or an honorarium. Experience also taught me that some individuals from each of those presentations would come to the center for personal therapy.

What Makes a Speaker?

Some people incorrectly assume that public speaking is standing at a formal dinner to say a few words about the guest of honor. Real public speaking is much more than that; it is GIVING your audience something valuable and meaningful, and it must have a few NECESSARY ingredients.

Some speakers assume that, if they have all the state-of-the-art gadgets, the equipment will make them stars. A musician might have all of the latest digital equipment to produce the music; but if the music lacks heart, the audience will know. Sure, a good amplifier will help a soft-spoken person to be heard better, but it will not make a better presenter.

Some assume that degrees are the only answer. Degrees surely command respect from the academic community and, usually, they are necessary to receive project grants from universities. Such formal education IS very valuable, but the best learning comes from real life experiences after graduation. Nor is age an important factor for success — there are plenty of old fools and young geniuses. At age fifteen, Edgar Cayce gave his first health discourse, Kahlil Gibran wrote his first version of *The Prophet*, and I guided my first past-life experience. What you have to say is more important than how old you are when you say it.

Having a lot of money will not make you a successful speaker. Money IS a tool; it can help with some things, but it is only a tool. The possession of money seldom solves problems of the heart, mind, or soul. The qualities that make a successful speaker are kindness, consideration, courage, and enthusiasm for the topic. Great speakers radiate a genuine respect for their audience's integrity and a desire to be of service to humanity — such are the necessary ingredients. This is termed "emotional intelligence" or "people skills" and makes all the difference, along with a passionate belief in what you are teaching.

What do YOU look for in a speaker? What does a speaker say or do that impresses you? THAT is probably what others will expect in you.

Take A Break

If you are like me, you'll never run out of great material during a presentation. If YOU need a break, rest assured that the audience will appreciate one, also. When you have been presenting a good deal of intense or "deep" material to a group, the members will need a break in order to lighten up and to assimilate the material — just as when eating a meal one needs ample time to digest it. No intelligent person will go from one meal directly into eating another meal without taking some time for digestion. Digestion is a tough job, and it takes a lot of guts. Speaking is an intense job, and it profits from a little playful rest!

A pause may be necessary as you regroup yourself or switch from one topic to the next. This brief break can be very useful for your audience. It allows time to reflect and to digest all the information that you have provided. On your side of the pause, things may seem more tense as though an eternity has passed since you spoke. Whatever you do, don't fill that pause with "umms" and "errs." Take a deep breath instead. Your audience will not mind. After all, you've been talking nonstop. Everyone needs a breath occasionally.

Assuming that you've been speaking for forty-five minutes or an hour, the best reason to break is, of course, for the bathroom! (It's rightly called "the pause that refreshes!") People do not like to admit that they HAVE TO GO, but watch **where** they go when you are considerate enough to give them that necessary break. Ask ahead of time where the facilities are so that you can point them out. You will need to let your audience know that this break is for you, too, and that there is time scheduled for audience sharing; otherwise, you will find yourself surrounded by people wanting to talk to you.

Be specific as to how long the break is and at what time you want to resume. It is easy to lose control of a group at break time. Reclaim it by announcing to everyone that it is time to get started again. Let them know that the information you have to offer is important, and they would want to get all of it. In all my years of speaking, only one person commented in an evaluation that I gave too many breaks. Thousands have **thanked** me (not in words, but in looks of sheer relief at break time). If people don't want to leave their places, you may suggest that they talk to the person nearest them or meditate upon what they have learned.

The next best method for a pause in the flow of your talk is to ask for any questions concerning what you have covered so far. This maneuver is good only if you are comfortable with your topic and if you can handle NOT having any hands raised. In that case, be prepared to fill the gap with something humorous. This line always works for me. "If you don't have a **real** question, you can make one up!" Humor works with my audiences because people are sometimes dubious of new research. Keep in mind that humor might be a saving grace for any topic. It can balance difficult concepts and all perspectives.

If done correctly, another useful "filler" or pause from your material is the insertion of a joke or a funny anecdote into your talk. People expect a joke near the beginning, so the placing of one well into your presentation is unexpected and may have even more humorous value. You reach people when guards are down, and this makes the story even funnier. Obviously, your joke should relate in some way to your general area of discussion.

A more indirect approach, should questions not arise from the audience, is: "Well, one question that a number of people might be concerned about is _____." Fill in that blank with some pertinent question that you would like for them to consider, a question that is crucial to the flow of your presentation. Then proceed to answer that question.

Oddly enough, the opposite situation can be a potential problem for a new speaker. If there are **too many** questions from the audience, you may answer a few and then politely limit questions by saying, "Okay. We'll take one more question for now, but we'll have plenty of time later for more questions and answers."

Another excellent way to fill the time during a pause is to tell a story, drawn from real life, that applies to your topic. The audience might not remember all of the facts and details of your speaking day, but they will remember a meaningful, touching, true story. It can be a sad story, a happy one, a story with an ironic twist, or it could take the form of a subtle, unconscious seed that will grow. To be most effective and believable, this story must be from your own life or that of a person close to you. A sad note here is that in the field of professional, motivational speakers I have actually heard some fictional stories presented as personal truth.

Storytelling helps people understand in their own way. Your story might concern an experience that you or someone else has had. By sharing it, your listeners can relate it to something going on in their own lives. By means of storytelling, they learn a lesson or they acquire an understanding that you wouldn't even have known was perfect for them. The bonus is that the same story will have a different meaning for each person. This is a great way to reach out to each individual on a more personal level. Jesus, Buddha, Confucius, and Milton Erickson chose to teach through storytelling. It worked for them!

Small Groups

As a speaker, I have many opportunities to listen to other speakers. As in all fields, some are excellent, others are good, and some are weak presenters. One technique that I have observed through the years is that of speakers who request that the audience break up into small groups for simultaneous discussion of an issue. Sometimes this approach can work exceptionally well, sometimes not. Speakers, who employ this technique successfully, bring the separate discussion highlights back to share with the whole group.

In my one-day workshops, I request the formation of small groups to engage in discussions during lunch time. I feel that this group work is beneficial because such informal sharing with companions helps to assimilate the work of the morning and still does not "eat into" the afternoon's schedule (only a mild pun intended).

People Skills

Mingling with individuals as they enter the room for your presentation creates a special bonding. If you can be near the door to introduce yourself, that's great. Your audience will feel welcomed and at ease with you. Remembering names creates a strong connection. Hopefully, they will get a name tag at registration.

The majority of people are visual. This means that they like to **look** while you are talking. It also means

*It is important to realize the commitment
made by deciding to become a public speaker.*

Artist: Jeffrey Winchester

that they tend to understand what you are saying better if they can "see" it. If you have no visual props, and individuals begin to count the buttons on your shirt, your words will fade from their minds. Take a blackboard, whiteboard, or flip chart that you can use periodically throughout the presentation. Personally, I prefer a dry erase whiteboard. It cleans up quickly and easily. Visual aids keep things rolling and break up the monotony. If you aren't a great artist, so what! Your efforts can be very comical and stress releasing. If you can bring in something to show, it's a real treat for your audience.

Commitment

When you speak to a group, you should give of yourself totally. This means letting them know why your topic is important. Boring your audience or not fully understanding your subject matter is a major obstacle. Remember, the participants will learn more than information about your topic. They will learn about you, just by your mannerisms and sincerity. Most audiences are filled with intuitive people, so don't even attempt to hide anything from them. Be honest and up front to win their trust. Recognize that what you have to tell them, they are there to hear.

It is important to realize the commitment you have made by deciding to become a public speaker. The words that you speak may be taken as gospel. Acknowledge the effect that your teaching could have on each person in that group. If this doesn't happen at the time, perhaps you have planted an idea which could surface later. Most of all, your actions speak much louder than your words.

As you are preparing to speak, a new creative process begins to flow within you. This is a wonderful gift and allows you to continue to grow and to learn in new ways. Inspirations will lead you to new projects, books, articles, and even new lectures. If your heart is in it, each presentation can be the beginning of much more fun and discovery to come. Always remember, you are doing this because you want to do it. Give yourself plenty of treats for every talk you give, for every job well done. Public speaking can help you to create your own exciting future.

Chapter Five
How to Work with Groups

Finding a Job — Or Inventing One!

Several times in my life I have had a "regular" job, that is, I worked for other people whose companies paid me for services rendered. I showed up for work on time, performed assigned tasks, and took home paychecks. This is an acceptable way to live, and I enjoyed the various jobs. But, for most of my adult life, I have worked for myself, which is one way of saying that I have chosen to be inventive, and to be willing to work extra hard. People who work for themselves usually put in long hours and work under difficult conditions. It is said that whereas an employee traditionally works the required eight hours a day, an entrepreneur will be motivated to work more than sixteen hours.

If you work for yourself, you'll appreciate your boss — hopefully! You will have a greater potential to make more money, you'll be able to set your own pace, and to work your own hours. If you are willing to work, you'll always have a job. The best future insurance is knowing that you are working **for** yourself.

In this age of electronic media dominating the airways, many people are appreciative of a live speaker with a timely topic. Various organizations need speakers as an incentive for members to attend their meetings, as a special gift to their regular membership, or as a form of continuing education. The need for excellent teachers will always be with us. Human beings want to learn, to grow, and to explore new horizons. You can be an important part of this on-going process!

Teaching

I am self-employed by giving workshops, and teaching others what I have learned in my field throughout many years of experience. There are many ways that people learn. As children, we accept the standard concept of school. Adults want to learn and to grow also, but their "school" environment is different. Some attend graduate school, others work from their own agenda and attend pertinent seminars, workshops, and specific training courses.

The word "seminar" implies a situation in which individuals address issues relating to a selected topic. Each speaker presents a separate aspect of the main topic. Although the speakers have limited time allotment, the audience can benefit from hearing even a brief presentation from a large variety of speakers.

The workshop, by contrast, has only one, or possibly, two speakers. Workshops require much more in-depth work with ample time devoted to one area of activity. A "work" shop implies some level of participation by the audience.

What Is a Workshop?

A workshop is an event or educational program that is more "hands on" or experiential than lectures. There is a particular level of integrated work, training, or exercises (whether of a physical, mental, emotional, or spiritual nature). In a workshop, people learn to **do** by **doing.**

Workshops can be magical. They are intended to unify random pieces into a whole that is clear and important. The workshop brings one's writing, speaking, research, **and** personality together into one package.

For example, consider the ingredients of flour, sugar, milk, butter, baking powder, and seasonings. Alone they aren't impressive, but when properly mixed, baked, and decorated, a cake is created! The sum total has an identity greater than the individual ingredients — synergy.

The finished product, your "cake" or workshop, is something you can serve with pride. An audience can partake of your creation with appreciation and enjoyment. The value and quality of your final product depends upon your knowledge and delivery. With time, you will refine your work, bringing it closer to perfection.

Who Can Give a Workshop?

Individuals from many walks of life give workshops. Presenters demonstrate a multitude of various skills. An academic degree is not required, but knowledge, sincerity, and experience in one's field certainly are necessary. A warm personality and a familiarity with groups are valuable, and a sense of humor adds greatly to the participants' ease in learning new skills.

Why are Workshops Given?

Many workshops are given in schools, trade schools, and colleges, but certain topics are simply too experimental to be available in any sort of university curriculum. Other topics go beyond the typical range of academia to include spiritual or emotional experiences. Specialized workshops are of interest to a limited number of professionals, like physical therapists or law enforcement personnel. Many are too technically advanced for the general public. Others are affiliated with churches or civic organizations.

If You Want to Get Started

If you want to attend a workshop, or if you would like to present one, there are three key questions to ask:
1. What is the workshop about?
2. What will participants learn or experience?
3. How will it help them?
    (What will they get for their money?)

I personally believe that many people would be excellent at giving workshops, but some will never know because they will never try. Don't believe that you shouldn't start giving classes until you have thorough knowledge of the field. Because new discoveries are being made everyday, I believe that I will never have thorough knowledge of my field. Many individuals — such as myself— have been active for decades in our calling and STILL are learning every day! I also believe that we actually learn MORE through teaching than in any other way.

Perhaps an excellent way to begin is to attend workshops given by others and observe the things THEY do that you like. Learn also from the things they do that you don't like. Brainstorm new ideas with friends and loved ones. What would you **really** like to teach others?

Imagine that you are ready to begin. You have a topic about which you want to teach others. Now, all you need

is information on preparing for the workshop —
working out the details. What kind of handouts do you
give? How do you attract an audience? Where will your
workshop be located? In order to give a successful workshop, all of the details must be thought through.

Local Programs

Start in your hometown and develop a program
for which you can handle all of the arrangements. You
will learn a great deal in the process. Later on, this
experience will help you to work with other people, in
other locations, to do the same job. In a local situation
you, most likely, will be the sole organizer; but when
you begin speaking in other cities (and countries!), you
will require a facilitator to organize those events. A
facilitator could be a friend or a professional
acquaintance. Often, he/she will be affiliated with a
sponsoring organization or group. The facilitator is vital
to the outcome. Enthusiasm and some previous
experience are major criteria for selecting the right
person for this job.

What Does a Facilitator Do?

1. Answers telephone inquiries
2. Conducts or arranges for a mailing
3. Orders the printing of handouts and promotional
    materials
4. Locates a meeting room
5. Receives early registrations

When your workshop is sponsored by a group, some
of the individual members are assigned specific tasks,
thus making arrangements easier for everyone.

Attracting Good Attendance at Your Workshop

Depending upon the topic and the speaker, people are willing to drive a couple of hours to attend a program. An interested person who lives close to the location is likely to attend the up-coming event. The most productive way to reach this prospective audience is by mail. This method is economical and effective when your mailing is followed by phone calls. Ask your prospects whether they received your material, and encourage them to tell their friends about the event. Telephone calls are most effective when a mailed notice is sent previously; therefore, a crisp, exciting, and attractive flyer is important!

Another ingredient crucial to success is a well defined mailing list. Local mailing lists are available. Lists relating to my area of expertise have been obtained from metaphysical bookstores, health food stores, and spiritual centers. Contact local businesses or centers that have interests compatible with your program topic and request a "one time" use of their mailing list.

It is obvious that the more specialized your list, the better the response it probably will generate. For example, the mailing list from a health food store could produce results for any topic related to health or fitness.

An effective method for establishing future mailing contacts is to work directly with local centers or branches of national organizations. They have access to extensive mailing lists and have gained experience by having sponsored various types of programs. Those facilitators will expect a percentage of your income; but if they do their parts well, the workshop attendance could be very large. Everyone benefits. Participants will be helped, the sponsoring organization will be pleased, and **you** will be happy. It's a "win-win-win" situation!

Other available sources of mailing lists are those obtained from brokerage houses — companies who own and rent , or sell, lists of individuals who have purchased items from specific catalogs, or who have membership in certain organizations. Perhaps you've noticed that if you take a membership in an organization for the preservation of nature, you will soon receive mailings from other similar organizations. Specialized mailing lists are valuable because you can use them to target a specific audience.

Finding a Workshop Location

The process of finding an excellent facility can be time-consuming but worthwhile. Some space is available at no cost such as a library conference room. Other locations require a nominal fee but offer greater flexibility. Various churches, synagogues, and spiritual centers have meeting rooms available. Community colleges often provide class-rooms for extra-curricular use, especially on Saturdays.

Standard commercial rates usually apply to locations such as hotels, motels, or civic organization meeting rooms. I have utilized all of the above, and I prefer the hotel/motel rooms because they are easy for people to find, have adequate parking, restroom facilities, and restaurants which are either in-house or nearby. If you choose this kind of location, be certain when scheduling your workshop that there is NOT a noisy event booked in an adjoining room.

One factor, vital above all others — more important than rental fees, more necessary than restrooms — is a quiet atmosphere. Unless your workshops are structured to be loud, fast-paced events, you'll want to locate a comfortable, serene area for your presentation. This might sound simple to arrange, but it isn't.

Somehow, when designing hotels, banquet rooms have become linked with kitchen facilities — supposedly to make it easier to shuffle the food in quickly! Although very logical in the planning stage, the reality is devastating for most workshop presentations. It's difficult to talk over the crashing of luncheon dishes. Food carts bouncing over tile floors is upsetting, to say the least!

My workshops contain guided reveries and self-hypnosis sessions. Mood and setting are very important. I always try to choose from among hotels, churches, meeting rooms, conference centers, or classrooms, where **quiet** is probable.

There are other factors to consider when choosing a location for lectures and workshops:

1. When the audience exceeds 25 people, a sound system is necessary. The lavaliere, or clip-on microphone, provides quality sound and allows freedom of movement for the speaker.

2. Comfortable seating is important. If good chairs are not available, participants should be advised to bring pillows or low-back supports.

3. Complimentary coffee, tea, and water should be available nearby. Participants should also be informed of vending areas or restaurants convenient for lunch.

4. Adequate restrooms should be available, so that the entire break period is not spent waiting in long, uncomfortable lines.

5. Since room temperature is a primary problem at most facilities, controls for adjustment should be available. Since individual preference might vary, participants should be advised to wear layered clothing that adjusts easily to changing temperatures.

6. Parking with handicap access should be convenient. Where there is a parking fee, include this information in the pre-registration packet.

7. A fairly low stage allows the presenter eye contact with the audience. Two lamps placed on stage add a peaceful, living-room touch.

8. A white-board is best for notes and illustrations. A flip chart is acceptable, but a white board with bright markers is better.

9. In consideration of public health, place all ashtrays some distance from any entrance to rooms or buildings, as smoke tends to blow in when a door is opened.

10. Pre-registration is vital to any successful program. This guarantees participants a place in the workshop, and it eliminates long lines at the door.

11. An evaluation form should be available to all workshop participants. Adequate room for personal comments as well as comments regarding the facility and the presenter should be included. Other questions to include are:

- How did you learn about this workshop?
- From where, or how far, did you travel to attend?
- Would you like to be on our mailing list?
- What speakers or workshop topics would you like presented in the future?

This information can be a valuable resource for future programs.

Publicity

For me, the biggest challenge as a workshop presenter is the development of a promotional strategy which maintains a balance between my individuality and my persona as a popular speaker, writer, and teacher. I try to avoid extremes of exalting myself or minimizing myself. After all, is it appropriate to seek self-glorification in this role? Or should an individual focus on the purposes and ideals of the true-self, rather than on the public-image? This dilemma must be resolved individually through self-analysis of one's own ideals, involvement, and integrity. Regardless of the response, this issue has a profound effect on public-image and publicity development.

Often individuals will approach me explaining, "I have a talent which I'm reluctant to publicize." They might have unique experiences with touch therapy, healing voices, musical skills, or other gifts. When I ask why they haven't made their talents available to humanity — a world in desperate need — they reply that they are afraid of being labeled "weird" or otherwise ridiculed. Why do people feel so fearful when so much good can be given to so many? I have always believed that to whom much is given, much is expected. Gifts and talents are to be used and shared. It is far better to try something positive and helpful than not to try at all. If you fail, just try again.

Why consider publicity development? People must know what you offer, where you are located, and how to contact you. Publicity is an accepted and necessary part of our world. Without some form of promotion, we fail to serve the needs in our communities. On the other hand, over-promoting yourself — self-aggrandizement — at the expense of other people is an equal failure.

After decades of self-evaluation, I believe that the proper balance in advertising is determined by the focus of the publicity and the ideals of each person. The goal is balance through rigorous self-honesty and constant evaluation of purposes and motivations. A presenter, regardless of the area of expertise, who focuses on SELF is self-centered and is not attuned to the ultimate goals. Proper balance between the exalting or minimizing of the self requires one to be alert constantly. The former is a hidden snare for the ego — a pitfall for the boastful and smug. Extreme humility, however, can be just as unwise an extreme as self-exaltation. Remember to keep a balance between magnifying and minimizing the self by focusing on your message. All promotional outreach should reflect your integrity and the primary goal of providing something beneficial for others.

So how do you promote yourself? You start right now; use whatever resources you have at hand. If you are a speaker, speak. If you are a writer, write. If you are a teacher, teach. Get busy! **Remember, no one can do your work quite the same way as you can.** Friends can help fine-tune your work and listen to your practice talks. Family can encourage you to success, but you must be the one to do the greater part of your promotional work.

Actually, on a long-term professional basis, no one will do your work for you unless you pay substantially to provide that service. If you expect others to do it for you, you'll probably have a long wait. Sometimes people are offered free promo perks and benefits through special contracts. In such arrangements, the promoters make it well worth their own efforts financially. The sad reality of life is that people will not make you their "cash cow" unless they own the pasture! It is just a fact of life — a fact of the present reality. Few people will do anything for you (except your mother) unless they get paid for it. This is not a bad situation; it just is. So, what do you do about that reality? You do as much as possible for yourself and trust that God helps those who help themselves! Where do you begin? You just do whatever you can to promote your work. Live simply, speak kindly, and boldly proclaim your truth with the fullness of your heart.

When many people come to the end of their lives they realize they missed opportunities to help others. Publicity and promotion are, simply, ways to let people know you can and are willing to help. You could pray piously every day to be of service to others, but it will not happen until you DO something about it. You have to let people know HOW you can help them and WHERE they can find you. They will tell others, and in time, you may receive invitations to speak to groups. Gradually, this process could evolve into seminars and workshops all over the country.

Roads to a better future are made by first clearing a path. The taking of small, easy steps with time and dedication is a key to successful accomplishments. Those practical and realistic procedures work! I know, because I have been using and refining them for decades. There is a positive outcome from all this effort. When the promotional work is accomplished, you will reap the rewards.

Personal growth and professional development are keys to success: share your learning, publish your research, and reach out to your community with integrity and ethical publicity. Your enthusiasm will engender interest from those you reach. When you promote the benefits of your specialty, you move from self to service. In other words, the message is more important than the messenger.

In my field, paid commercial advertising is usually NOT cost effective; but FREE ads, or listings in a Community Calendar are acceptable. I have found that the most effective way to publicize a workshop is by direct mailing. At first, you will need to acquire a mailing list; however, in time, you will develop your own. Whenever you speak, ask the participants to **print** their names, addresses, and ZIP CODES, and you can compile your own list.

Once again, when using direct mail, it bears repeating that your advertising flyer is of vital importance! Use your writing skills to produce a good advertising brochure to describe your workshop. State clearly how participants will benefit from the program. Test different titles and approaches that maximize the benefits offered. Create short articles related to your field and make sure that they are published in conjunction with your program(s).

Cost

For your first few programs, keep tuition reasonable. In fact, this is a good policy to follow for ALL subsequent programs as well! People appreciate high-quality presentations at reasonable cost. With time, patience, and experience, people will hear about you and will tell their friends. The topic of money is such an arbitrary one that I cannot suggest a set rate. Costs of conference rooms, printing, promotion, and various other expenses all figure into determining those fees. A survey of the tuitions charged by other area presenters can be advantageous. Costs and tuitions vary widely from city to city and from presenter to presenter.

Designing Workshop Materials

Designing a workshop can be one of the most creative and productive opportunities of your life. You can incorporate into it all the very best sources of study and the finest skills you have mastered. A great workshop

may be more powerful than a book and more memorable than a speech because it can touch the lives of
participants in the deepest and most meaningful method
known — "hands on" experience!

Here is a list of procedures for designing workshop
materials. They can be adapted to fit your own needs.
The object is to bring a "package" together wherein
the components fit into a whole, and the whole is greater
than its separate parts.

Essential materials include:

1. Title
2. Logo
3. Outline of the workshop and its activities
4. Brochure or flyer explaining the workshop
5. Workshop manual (or handouts)
6. Graphics or artwork

Optional materials:

7. Stationery, business cards
8. Posters
9. Sale items (books, booklets, audio tapes,
    videotapes, etc.)

Let's analyze the above items individually,
remembering that, eventually, they will dovetail into a
complete package.

1. Title: Any workshop absolutely requires a title.
To discover a working title, simply list about ten best
phrases which accurately describe your program.
(You may use favorite titles from previous talks which
you have given.) Approach friends or acquaintances
telling them that you are surveying the selection of a
title for your program. Ask them to choose their
favorite, but do NOT allow them to see the votes that
other titles have received because it could influence
their choices.

After polling perhaps twenty individuals, you will notice that one or two titles received the majority of votes. One of those titles might be your best choice.

2. Logo: A logo is a visual design or word group which graphically reminds people of a product. Originally, a logo was a trademark but now it is much more. It symbolizes the company, the product, and its IMAGE. If you wonder just how valuable a logo is, drive down any street where businesses offer their services and notice the countless signs displayed by gas companies, restaurants, shops, etc. The logo is **the** symbol of a company and many are recognized internationally. They can transcend verbal languages!

Logos are vital to product recognition. Your logo will be valuable to you, so take special care in designing it. Examine the work of logo designers and be willing to pay for that service. Keep your logo simple and clear. Whether a logo is designed methodically or is an inspiration, or both, it is vital to your work and to your image. It can prove to be more influential than the title. It IS your image!

Sue Jones, a gifted graphic artist, has created most of my logos as well as other artwork for my books. I asked Sue to explain the process she uses to design a logo. Read carefully, for she outlines a procedure that might be helpful to you.

Designing a Logo (written by Sue Jones)

"How does an inspired work evolve? Sometimes, it just "pops" into your mind. Other times, it requires incubation time. Many times, just the act of doing something will start the process flowing.

The logo used for *Healing the Past, Building the Future* is an example of inspired artwork. My thought process went something like this:

Question 1:   What is healing?
Answer 1:   Laying on of hands, light, love, …
Question 2:   How is the past healed?
Answer 2:   Reconciling feelings from the heart? (Sometimes an answer is another question.)
Question 3:   What is building the future?
Answer 3:   You build from the bottom up. Could that be a triangle or pyramid shape? Something that directs the healing light into a pattern or shape?
Question 4:   How do all the aspects fit together into one logo to depict this workshop?
Answer 4:   I don't know. I'll set it aside for a while.

For this particular logo, there was no agonizing. The questions listed above were answered very quickly. Not long afterwards, the logo just "popped" into my head. I sat down, looked at my hands, sketched them, and added the other aspects of the logo. It wanted to happen very quickly, so I just let it out. I could tell it was inspired — it seemed special.

Usually, I have to struggle before the idea comes. I have to sit and make lists and sketches of everything relating to the idea. I try to discover how the text will fit into the image to become a consolidated piece. Finally, I put it aside and work on other projects.

It always seems later, when I'm doing something totally unrelated, an idea or two will come to me. It is only after I have done my rational thinking that an intuitive idea takes shape. Sometimes in the middle of the night or during a dream, it comes to me. Sometimes, a change in scenery helps — a drive in the mountains or to another city. Maybe writing in my journal or going for a walk. It seems, I have to disassociate myself from the original ideas to gain access to the intuitive.

To bring out the inspiration, I first have to lay the groundwork in my rational mind. I have to make my written list of ideas and words relating to the logo. One idea or word, however, is not a logo — it is usually a culmination of many ideas brought together when it all "clicks." That is where intuition takes over. It takes both sides of the mind to bring about the inspired. It seems the rational gets the intuitive part moving." [Note: Sue Jones' address is listed in the appendix.]

Artist: Sue Jones

HEALING THE PAST
BUILDING THE FUTURE

The logo used for the workshop of the same name.

3. Outline: Make an outline of the workshop activities or make a schedule of the day. The subtopics will be material with which you are familiar, generally consisting of articles you have previously written and talks you have presented. ALL workshops should have hands-on exercises or projects. They may be interspersed with talks and informal lectures.

Ideally, a workshop builds sequentially. It opens with a theme, incorporates pertinent activities, and progresses to a meaningful conclusion.

4. Brochure and/or flyer: Brochures and flyers are necessary to promote and to define a workshop. It might be best to give the workshop a test-run before paying to have your brochure designed and printed. To test-run a program, gather friends together or offer a free program through your local library. The test-run will teach you proper timing. The audience doesn't want useless "filler" nor do they want to be told that you ran out of time before you could give your entire presentation.

When presentation scheduling is set, contact a graphic design person, or your printer, concerning the layout of the flyer or brochure. Again, this is not the time to cut corners, as promotional materials form the first impression which people will receive regarding your program and YOU.

Place the logo, as well as your name, in a prominent position on your brochure. Make sure that your address and phone number are CLEARLY visible. Acquire a clear photo of yourself for use on the flyer. Research clearly demonstrates that a flyer **with** a photo is read more frequently than one without. People want to see with whom they are dealing, so USE your photo.

Obtain printing estimates from three or more printers and ask to see some recent samples of their work. When judging printed materials make sure the ink coverage is not too light and the brochure is trimmed and folded properly. The lowest estimate is not always the best deal, nor is the most expensive. The level of cost might not reflect the best value. Compare cost to quality, and appearance to promptness.

If there is a particular business with printed materials you like, ask which printer was used. Often, you will learn if the printer delivered a quality job on time. When requesting an estimate from the printer, mention the source of the recommendation — sometimes it helps to create good will in the beginning.

Writing the advertisement flyer for your workshop is very different from other writing tasks. It must reflect a degree of excitement and enthusiasm in order to attract an audience and to persuade people to attend. You are asking people to take a full day away from their week or weekend, away from family and friends, to come and to do some WORK! The enticement must be appealing — but without hype or pressure.

One or two sentences relating to the theme must state the key purpose and definition of your workshop. Bring out the high points of your program and the important information that people will receive from the presentation.

Tell people HOW the workshop is valuable to them and WHY! Keep your flyer short and easy to read. Individuals who attend workshops tend to be outgoing or "hands on" sort of people. They come for the **experience**.

After writing your material, read it over as if you were receiving it in the mail. Does it excite you? Does it make **you** want to attend? Does it contain items of personal importance helpful to you? Can it teach you something valuable? If not, go back and rework your

HEALING THE PAST
BUILDING THE FUTURE

HEALING THE PAST — BUILDING THE FUTURE explores the whole spectrum of human healing. This comprehensive one-day workshop introduces holistic healing techniques that go beyond the limits of the physical body and into the heart of a deeper reality. You will be given valuable tools to help heal yourself physically, mentally, emotionally, spiritually, and even financially.

Schedule of Events...

Early morning

Healing the Present
- Healing is for life
- Healing potential/ healing talents
- Discovering your gifts

Experience...
  A guided session based on the work of Dr. Milton H. Erickson, *Discovering the Healer Within — Healing the Healer*

Mid-morning

Healing the Past
- Past-life regression
- Patterns of hurt or healing
- Wisdom of your heart's memory

Experience...
  A dialogue to integrate past-life self with present-life self.

Healing the Future
- A glimpse into your future
- Utilizing future-vision to evaluate your present life.

Experience...
  A guided group session, *Your Extraordinary Journey Through Time.*

Lunch ... small sharing groups and discussion.

Early afternoon

Traditional & Innovative Healing
- Hydrotherapy
- Humor as it heals naturally
- Healing through travel

Experience...
  Embracing your Eternal Child — the incredible healing power of love.

Late Afternoon

Healing from the Higher Self
- Gifts from the superconscious mind

Experience...
  An exercise for inspired writing or drawing.

This is an example of a workshop outline or Schedule of the Day. This is my one-day workshop, entitled Healing the Past — Building the Future.

Soul Lessons & Forgiveness

LIFE PATTERNS are the relationships, the thoughts, the problems that we never seem to get beyond — those cycles of behavior that repeat themselves over and over again in our lives. Although many people are aware of such cycles, few realize how they create them, or how they can use them as opportunities for growth and learning. Discover new and creative ways to access those skills, talents, abilities, and emotions that are unique to each of us.

Schedule of Workshop Events...

Early morning

Life Patterns
• Positive and challenging patterns
• Deciphering the patterns of your past
• Designing your destiny
• Experience an inner adventure: **Ideals — The Authentic You**

Mid-morning

Your Soul's Remembrances
• Past-life exploration procedures
• Soul lessons and progressions
• Forgiveness as the key
• Experience an inner adventure: **Past-life Regression**

Lunch ... small sharing groups and discussion.

Early afternoon

Discovering Your Inner self
• How you have gained or lost
• Love, sexuality, and spirituality
• Holy poverty!
• Monks, warriors, and other extremes
• Experience an inner adventure: **Pack Your Bags with the Treasures of Your Past**

Late Afternoon

Strategies for Success
• Charting your soul's journey
• Journal writing — writing to learn
• Creating a personal sanctuary
• Your spiritual retreat

An example of my **Life Patterns** *workshop schedule.*

text! Rewrite once again. Your flyer MUST "grab" people and persuade them to come! It is your best promotion.

5. Workshop manual or handouts: Handouts are intended to be used appropriately to complement your material — not to be read aloud. You can provide free handouts to participants by adapting parts of your previously written materials.

Your investments in creative writing can now pay interest and dividends! A good workshop utilizes printed materials for participants. Begin with simple one-page flyers. Later, those pages or handouts can be adapted into little booklets or pamphlets by folding the pages and stapling. A published article you have written on any related topic may be photocopied to make a free handout; however, be sure to provide credit showing when, where, and by whom the selection was published.

My own handouts evolved in this very manner. I re-worked and improved them through the years until a manual evolved. I found artists who contributed illustrations which added to the appeal of my material. A local printer might be able to assist you with a layout or might recommend a person who could help you with such technical tasks or with the possibility of artwork.

Start with the materials that you already have, perhaps some articles that you have written, whether published or unpublished. Have the articles photo-copied or inexpensively "rapid printed" as free handouts. Always be sure that your name, address, phone number, and your logo are printed on **all** workshop materials.

If you are just beginning and have not yet accumulated your own materials, you may use a photocopy of a relevant journal or magazine article, as long as appropriate credits and permission are given (author, title of article, magazine name, and date of issue). Your own material, however, is much more effective and more meaningful for your group.

Perhaps, at first, your manual is only a few articles or handouts stapled together or grouped in an inexpensive folder. As time goes on and you receive income from your workshops, you can pay to have the materials set and printed in a more attractive format. A booklet is more valuable to attendees, who'll probably keep it for future reference. Often, photocopies are soon discarded.

Some presenters prefer to charge a fee for their manual as one way to recoup their printing costs. I prefer to incorporate the cost into the registration. This way, the participants are assured of something tangible to take home with them. It is also good advertising since everytime they pick up their manuals they will be reminded of your workshops. Any friends that borrow their manuals might write to request more information from you.

6. Artwork: Visuals are always important for any workshop because 70% of all people are primarily visually oriented. Unless you possess drawing and artistic skills, it is better to pay a commercial artist to produce your materials. Find an artist who can create clear, easy-to-understand images, relevant sketches, diagrams, or cartoons.

7. Stationery (optional): Letterheads, envelopes, and business cards could be printed at the same time as your brochure. This procedure saves quite a lot of money, especially if you are using colored inks. The secret is to coordinate all items to create an attractive, cost-effective package. Be **sure** to use colors. Use the SAME color(s) throughout your materials, because it will add continuity to your package, and it is important for audience recognition.

Do not pay a high price for expensive paper. With a less expensive paper, you will be able to print a larger quantity for the same price as the more expensive paper. Ask your printer which papers they keep in stock. Those papers are often bought in bulk which makes them less expensive. Sometimes, printers will have paper left from another job and will discount it just to get it off of their shelves. There is no waiting period for paper that is already in stock — it doesn't have to be ordered and delivered to the printer.

8. Posters (optional): A poster? Yes! This idea came to me unexpectedly, and it has proved to be a valuable addition to workshop promotion. Using a favorite piece of artwork that has been produced for you, have a small or medium-size poster printed. The cost is minimal, but the advantage is extraordinary. You could advertise FREELY in local stores simply by printing with a magic marker the date, time, and place of your upcoming event directly onto the poster itself. Give a contact phone number, also.

Copies of your poster can be sold at the workshop, or a free copy can be given to attendees to take home. I must confess, with a certain amount of gratitude, that I have seen my posters hung proudly in the most unexpected places! People appreciate beautiful artwork and will admire it for years.

9. Sale items (optional): Financially, it is wise to have items for sale following a workshop or any program that you give. After the presentation, people are excited about continuing their work and they want more "tools" to bring home. Many wish to share the information with family and friends.

Obviously, if you have already produced booklets, books, videos, or cassette tapes, be sure to have them for sale. Near the close of the program, hold them up for people to see, and point out their display in the room.

If you have not yet produced any items for sale, allow me to suggest the easiest and perhaps most cost-effective item to manufacture: cassette tapes. Find a local musician who has a home studio, or locate a small commercial studio where you could record a master tape of the highlights of your program. Later, you can record tapes adding related materials to enhance and to accentuate your original program.

Once you possess a master recording, you can produce additional copies on a cassette duplicating machine or you can have the studio make copies. A fair profit margin can be made, and the entire "tape project" could require as little as a month to complete. A book, on the other hand, could take a year or more to create in its final form.

With some planning, well-designed materials can help make a workshop a very memorable event. The participants will be able to take home a "piece" of the presentation as a reminder of the day. They will have material to share with others after the end of the presentation.

Ending the Day: What is an Autograph all About?

I do not know the origin of autographing a book. Why do people want an author to sign their copies of a book? Some people seem to desire and to appreciate an author's signature, and it has become a great tradition. Why deny them such a simple pleasure? I happily sign my books at the **close** of the workshop presentation, usually at about 5:00 p.m.

After each workshop, there are tasks to be completed. The books and tapes must be packed into boxes, evaluations must be collected, sometimes chairs must be stacked, and a general clean-up undertaken. Usually, at this time, I am busy signing autographs. People line up and wait patiently. I am always amazed that they seem so delighted with this post-workshop ritual. (Whoever said that we didn't have rituals in our society!) Almost 30% of the audience participates. Some have even purchased a copy of every sale item!

Having been an antique dealer for many years, I am aware that signed books are much more valuable than those not bearing an author's signature, and first editions have far more value than subsequent printings. But more than the dollar value involved, I believe that a person simply likes the fact that the author wrote a little note in his or her book and dated the signing. This makes an encounter with the author personal and meaningful.

Seminars: Give the People What They Want

Life changes. Every year, every season, there are new topics that are of interest to people — "hot" topics. Who knows for sure why this is! Perhaps it's the media that brings to life or inspires certain issues, perhaps people become intrigued with specific ideas, or perhaps it is a combination of both. In my three decades of work in this field, I have seen numerous "hot" topics come and go, almost like fads. Some topics, tried and true, become an important part of one's work. Others are seldom heard of again.

If you wish, you may list those areas of interest as they arise, and design your programs to include the most popular topics. Possibly, you will do well with this approach, but my procedure is entirely different.

Over the years, I have dealt with two main domains of work, and I continue to stay within them. As my topics became popular, I gained more notice. I was established in two areas: Self-Hypnosis and Past-Life Exploration. The advantage of remaining with one or two familiar interests is that your material becomes quite good, for you are dedicated to those subjects, and you keep abreast of your field. You become an authority in that area.

On the other hand, you can experiment with a bit of everything. You can give timely introductory programs on current topics. You can become a general spokesperson for a **wider** field.

Another approach is to introduce entirely new topics — topics that you want to share with people but for which there are no precedents. For instance, in my book *Life Patterns*, I introduced three topics that rarely had been discussed. There were few other books or articles available on those subjects at the time. I wrote *Life Patterns* because I felt that there was a need to acknowledge the importance of three topics: Life Patterns, Soul Lessons, and Forgiveness. Time has shown that many, many people ARE interested in those subjects.

My three new topics were a by-product of my past-life regression work, and so I moved naturally into new territory without abandoning my original work. I **added** to it. Remaining within a certain area of expertise might "type cast" you, but it also allows you to become known as an authority in that field. As I do, you may expand upon your work at any time. It adds immeasurably to the overall scope of what you are able to accomplish.

To discover what interests people, **ask them**! Attend programs and ask members of the audience what they liked about the program and what they did not like. Ask what is of importance to them in their own lives and what they would like to hear discussed and presented in other programs. Interview enough people to make this survey worthwhile, but be sure to realize that what the public says it wants, and what it actually will make the effort to attend, sometimes is very different.

Usually, people want to be given information that can be of help to them personally. A doctor might discuss healing to little avail, but, more successfully, might demonstrate a few simple exercises that can be continued at home. A speaker might discuss various theories of reincarnation, or could skip the theories and ask people to explore memories within themselves that are relevant and pertinent to present-life situations. A Native American might talk about the theory of dreams but, instead, could teach groups how to weave their own dream catchers. You get the point! Involve your participants personally and give them something, tangible or intangible, to take home with them, something to remember you and your presentation by, something timely and meaningful to them individually.

People **want** meaningful and helpful experiences. They like projects to take home for continued work, and they want to come away with material to show their friends what was involved in the workshop. People like to feel connected to the presenter; therefore, I offer my audience the chance to write to me at any time in the future. And, I answer **all** letters. I ask people whether they would like to be added to my mailing list, and I strive to send them one mailing each year.

Four Things an Audience Does Not Want:

1. A speaker who mumbles or strays from the microphone.

2. When the speaker wanders down the blind alley of meaningless tangents. Keep focused on the subject.

3. Long lists of facts (boring stuff). Present your factual information in the form of brochures or handouts; leave it out of your talk.

4. The greatest transgression any speaker can commit is to read a speech to an audience. Today's sophisticated audiences **already** know how to read.

A Helpful Hint

Calling friends and acquaintances to ask them to help you to facilitate a workshop or a seminar is not a good approach. It could place your friends in the uncomfortable position of having to refuse, and they might feel pressured.

It is better to ask friends and acquaintances whether they know of ANYONE who could facilitate for you. Approached in this fashion, they are asked more to assist you in finding someone **else** who could help out. Some will have no "leads" for you; others will come up with excellent prospective facilitators.

Later, write or call those leads and explain your work. Say that they were recommended by a friend. Most of your friends will not mind if you use their names as references. (In this situation, you are only asking a friend of a friend for help.) Some of my very best facilitators have been discovered in this indirect fashion. When contacted about facilitating, some people will refuse. Some will agree to work with you, because they see the idea appealing and profitable. Most of all, by consenting to be your facilitator, such people will be instrumental in bringing wonderful programs into their areas and, thereby, being of service to many other people.

Teaching Without Charge

In the early stages of your career, it is important that you seek out any group or organization that would want to engage you as an unpaid presenter. You offer your services at no charge because this will be good practice for you, and it will help to develop your skills. Do not be hesitant to teach, even without pay, for each opportunity promotes your career. It's an easy and practical way to enter the field of presenting professionally. At times, you might want to test-run a workshop by offering it free to local audiences. Most people are very happy to suggest their favorite organization or civic group as the possible recipient of a free program. Keep a list of those attending your presentation as the beginning of your **own** future mailing list.

Remember, no one will respond if you don't write. No one will answer the door if you don't knock. No one will say "yes" if you don't take the initiative and call. Entrepreneurs realize that for every "yes" answer, there are frequent "no" answers. This is playing the odds in life. The more that you ask, the more "yes" responses you'll receive!

A Word about Videos

Videos are rapidly becoming an important communication tool. I strongly advise that you learn about and make use of this new media as a part of your creative expression. It's important that you practice writing because you'll need good material and scripts to incorporate into your videos. Then practice speaking because you'll need to be comfortable in front of an audience and a camera. Present workshops — you'll need this experience also. When you have become proficient in those areas, then you can open doors to electronic and visual frontiers.

Important tips for video success are:
1. Your material must be visual or readily adaptable to visual comprehension.
2. You'll need effective scripts and dialogue. (You can adapt some written material that you already have done.)
3. Stay in your general field of expertise.
4. The more widely you are known, the better your sales will be, so work hard to keep **yourself** visible.
5. Work with people currently involved with the media.

A number of years ago, I took my first step into the world of videos. Friends came for the weekend and brought their new equipment which was still packed away in its original box. More for fun than anything else, we decided to make a regression video. They asked me to speak, explaining the procedure and then to demonstrate by holding two regression sessions.

Nothing was rehearsed; this was an extemporaneous production! We experimented as we worked. The regressions came out well, but the technical apparatus and the resulting product was only fair. A local TV repair shop duplicated about twenty copies, and I offered them for sale through a small classified ad.

All twenty copies sold immediately, and I realized that there was a market for videos, but unfortunately, there was not a studio convenient for continued production. I now offer a professional video, and I plan to produce more. I also allow people to film, free of charge, any of my workshops and talks; but the finished product is usually of a poor quality. A professional video presentation requires strong lighting, clear sound, proper staging, and appropriate editing — elements essential for a fine finished product.

When producing a video, accurate material content is even more important than the technical aspects of filming. Applied information contained in a video must be accurate. For example, a friend purchased a video about how to make money by giving "how to stop smoking" seminars. Such seminars are quite common all around the country, and they involve a large attendance and a two-hour hypnosis program.

Unfortunately, the video spokesperson presenting this seminar painted an unrealistic picture of the program's potential financial success. He gave information that exaggerated projected income levels. Unaware, my friend purchased the video, carefully followed the instructions, took out expensive ads, rented a large hotel conference room in the heart of New York City, and then — nothing! Only a few people responded to his advertising. SOME-THING definitely was lacking. My friend learned a sad lesson about so-called video courses and easy money.

Radio and TV

As your career progresses, you might be offered — or you could create! — opportunities for television and radio outreach. Each has advantages and disadvantages of which you should be aware. Radio is the simplest to access, and it is a good introduction to media outreach. TV, although more difficult to access, does allow people to see as well as to hear you.

My experience in the field has given me opportunities to be on both radio and television, nationally and internationally. I have been fortunate to have been featured on television in three countries, as well as on "Primetime," a nationally syndicated program here in America.

Although I have always been treated with respect regarding those appearances, media presentations are restricted by time limits and are interrupted by scheduled advertising. If your experience with the media is characterized by kindness and consideration, be grateful. If it should be indifferent or even harsh, don't be upset. Such treatment is often the norm. Media loves controversy and can be manipulative to that end.

Theoretically, freedom and integrity of the press is a sacred tenet of our nation's ideology. But in reality, the situation is often very different. True freedom of the press is guaranteed only to those people who own the presses, or the radio and television networks. Don't let this frighten you, but be awake to the situation.

Technically, the media has no overt political power. Actually radio and television do exert a very real control and influence upon our nation and the world. The range and the power of media are vast.

Don't be Afraid to Ask!

The world of electronic communications is too extensive for one person to master alone. As with writing, speaking, and planning workshops, you'll need help. To fill the gap in areas where you might need help, ask for it!

When you ask others for help, some will be pleased to assist. Soon, you will accumulate a few dedicated co-workers. Find ways to reward those individuals for their help. This gesture does not have to be monetary. Respond to each helper in an appropriate way.

For example, writing is NOT my strength, and I candidly admit my limitations. English is my second language and it shows. The act of writing is somewhat satisfying but not thrilling. Often, I even wonder whether you, the reader, will be able to follow what I wish to convey; therefore, I ask the assistance of others in polishing and refining my work so that it flows and is readily understandable. In this way, I have established a number of wonderful working relationships.

Public speaking, on the other hand, is very different. I eagerly await each opportunity. It's as though my entire life has been preparing me to share and to be with an audience. Speaking is exciting and fun — it's what I love to do.

Identify your strengths and use them. The more you use them, the stronger they will become. It is wiser to utilize your natural gifts to the fullest, rather than to struggle for development in weaker areas.

Your Rewards

If what I have suggested seems to entail extensive work and constant attention, I can assure you that the rewards are great. You will help to teach, to encourage, and to inspire hundreds — perhaps many thousands — of people to reach their highest goals and ideals. It is **definitely** worth the effort.

You might have to pay for the professional services of those who assist you with the materials that you finally produce. Successful workshops eventually will bring a return of your investment with substantial gains.

A workshop is a golden opportunity to bring together the BEST of your writing, speaking, and research into a complete package. Combine the very finest of your materials and offer them neatly wrapped and beautifully presented. It is the gift of yourself.

Best of all, those who attend your presentations will receive your material through ALL modes of learning. That is, visual people will see you and your drawings, charts, and graphics. Auditory people will hear you speak and listen to their own inner counsel. Kinesthetic people, who learn through hands-on approaches, will experience profoundly what you teach. Each type of person learns through a certain avenue of response. A workshop environment is ideal because it teaches people at ALL levels.

As a professional presenter in your field, you will be a representative, a motivational role model. As such, it is vital that you keep balance, composure, adaptability, and, most importantly, a sense of humor. Those characteristics are essential to success. Give yourself plenty of time to grow into your field, but don't keep stalling. Do not delay action by waiting too long, for fear of making mistakes, or by thinking that just "one more class" or "one more degree" will make all the difference.

Everyone makes mistakes. You accept your mistakes as opportunities for making corrections. Learning from mistakes is the real issue — as well as the risk of not learning from them. In fact, some of the worst errors eventually led people on to their greatest successes and accomplishments. The only real failure is to refuse to learn and to grow from an experience. Don't be afraid to begin. Just reach out and touch your future. You will learn valuable lessons through struggle and hard work. All change requires courage. Adapting to change builds wisdom and clarifies your true purpose and destiny.

Chapter Six
Workshops That Work

From Theory to Practice

There are many roads that lead to any destination. No one road is the only, or best road for all travelers. The information and techniques I am sharing in this book are obviously tailored by my experience. It is a travelogue of the roads that I have taken and the destination I have reached.

Your vision of the journey might not coincide with the steps and sequences I described. That is natural and normal. Your journey and destination could reach far beyond my greatest hopes. Perhaps your dream is in the accomplishment of only one aspect of the journey.

Be There Early

To help your presentation flow, you need to feel comfortable in the room that you are using. Go there early or even the day before your engagement. Let yourself just experience the room. Take a deep breath and feel your energy expanding out into the room. Imagine this room full of people, laughing and learning. Picture yourself at the front of the room feeling confident and sharing with the audience. **Expect** that everyone will have a good time. This visual imagery can be very helpful when creating a new situation — it's a constructive use of your imagination.

Check out the room as if you were a member of the audience. Are the seats properly arranged for the best overall view? Will they be able to hear you easily? Make sure the microphone and audio systems are functioning properly. I suggest a clip-on mike as this frees your hands for broader gestures and for utilizing your visual aids. Are the visual aids ready? Run through all arrangements in your mind and be sure that everything is accessible. Make a list to check things that need to be done. Small details left undone are things that can pull your attention away from your presentation. You will want to be as focused as possible.

Get Centered

As the time arrives, you are excited and knowledgeable about your topic. You have practiced. Your outline is prepared. Small details are in order. The room is full of people. As you look around, you see your audience already looking bored, bewildered, or lost. This is not at all the way you visualized it! What could possibly be wrong with the people? SO WHAT HAPPENED? They are waiting for you! Take charge and jump into it with all the enthusiasm and confidence that you have. Thank them for coming and tell them a little about yourself, or something humorous. Their interest will pick up. Before you know it, everyone will be having a great time.

On a personal note, it took a few different audiences before I realized a great truth. When people sit, waiting for a talk or program, they sometimes look bored. They actually are not bored. Of course not. They paid a good sum of money to attend; many traveled a long way; they WANT to be there. They want to hear and to learn. They probably don't even realize that they look bored.

Your audience wants to hear everything you have to say, so speak slowly and clearly. Pace yourself. You have rehearsed this whole thing, and there is no need to feel rushed. If you find that there is extra time because your presentation went too quickly, ask for questions or share another story. **Always** schedule time for questions. Participants sometimes ask you something that has nothing to do with your topic! Or perhaps, there is something that they want to share with you. Those are great signs. This means that you let them get involved so deeply that they feel confident and comfortable with you. When appropriate, let your answers be humorous. Everybody loves spontaneity. Have fun!

My Speaking Day

I've discussed the process of designing materials and consolidating programs. Now, we shall move into the exciting work of presenting a workshop. As a model, I shall explain my speaking day. As you read, envision how YOUR speaking day would be. What would you do similarly? What would you change or adapt to your style? What would you do that is completely different?

On a workshop morning, I get up at 6 a.m. to begin the preliminaries. There are many details which will vary, depending on the hotel or conference center at which I am speaking. As I refer to this typical day, imagine a hotel conference room and how **your** workshop might be.

Artist: Kathye Mendes

On weekends, most hotels retain only a skeleton staff.

Generally, I make presentations on Saturdays when most hotels retain only a skeleton staff, so I locate the person supervising the conference area to confirm and to coordinate the details. I make sure that the room is open and that the chairs, registration tables, and product display areas are set-up. I carefully check the sound system, and always carry my own lavaliere microphone. Next, I turn on all of the lights, even before people arrive.

It's more personal and welcoming to come into a nicely illuminated room. I make certain that signs are posted to direct program participants to the conference room.

Then, as the program coordinators arrive, I go over the product inventory with the sales coordinator. I provide the registrar with free manuals which give the participants reading materials before the program begins. Next I write notices and information on the chalkboard.

As people begin to arrive, I give them a special welcome for being early. I assure them that we will start on time. If they have arrived very early, I direct them to a coffee shop or vending area if they are interested. When all of the preliminaries are completed, I go for breakfast. I remain nearby but not in the foreground.

Prior to the presentation, I meet with the individual from the sponsoring organization who will introduce me to the audience and provide details to ensure that the introduction does not merely repeat what is said in the printed materials. When this individual is a personal acquaintance or has attended one of my previous presentations, the introduction is more personal, which is especially nice. I gratefully accept this introduction and acknowledge the sponsoring organization. A genuine smile and a relaxed stance are also very important.

In earlier years, I was nervous but experience has alleviated that anxiety. Now, I am eager and ready for action. When I need to "get a feel" for an audience, I ask how many of them have heard me speak previously. Then, I ask if today's topic is new for anyone or if they have general knowledge of the field. This helps me to tailor my presentation to the group — modifying the material as needed.

I ensure that all participants have workshop
manuals, and I remind them to keep the manuals for
future reference. Next, I review the entire day's schedule,
taking special note of breaks and certain activities of
interest. Now comes the most important part of the day.
I ask the participants to join me in a moment of silence.
Then, my inner guidance leads me in a prayer. This
prayer is not memorized but one which seems to flow
easily, as prayers will do. Such prayers are different for
each occasion and can provide a special direction for
each group and presentation.

I make it clear that the workshop involves doing very
practical inner work — that it is not a day of mere
theorizing. I try to give my audience as much material
as possible without rushing. I strive to impart to all
participants the most valuable information that I can in
a way that they will understand. I offer to send to each
person present, at no cost, source materials and/or
references to any material presented. I call special
attention to my address printed on their manuals and
written on the board.

I hold two ideals in mind as I make a presentation.
First, I strive to teach what is most important about my
topic in order to provide valuable information. Second,
I make a sincere effort to lead the most meaningful,
experiential sessions possible for all participants. This
two-part approach appeals to varied learning styles of
individuals. The lecture provides an auditory learning
experience. The guided reveries stimulate intrapersonal
discovery. Most people relate primarily through visual,
auditory, or kinesthetic senses. I strive to use words and
pictures that resonate with each of those receptors. I
arrange the day to appeal to all participants by
employing a variety of hands-on experiences.

Humor is the "fun stuff" that makes a day memorable. I must admit that some jokes are worked into my presentation, but the most humorous material is always spontaneous. When people laugh, the door is opened to even more humor — and the participants will create their own! Soon, everyone begins to have fun. Often, during the question and answer period, comical answers will come out, unplanned and unexpected. This part of the workshop is very exhilarating.

Mailing Lists — Your Most Valuable Asset!

When you start your workshop business, some prospects will express only a little interest, while others will show great enthusiasm concerning your visit to their area. Keep a special list of all those who express any interest whatsoever in having you speak. This list will become your most important and valuable work-shop resource. I maintain two such lists.

One list is comprised of "study groups" who have expressed an interest in my work. When a **study group** sponsors your program, the members usually will have dedicated helpers involved in the workload of managing the details. (A disadvantage of this situation is that decisions have to go to the entire group for consensus, which can sometimes lead to differing opinions and delays. A well-organized group appoints a coordinator who mediates for the group.) The second list contains the names of **individuals** who already have sponsored one of my workshops, or who have indicated a desire to do so in the future. Individual sponsors have more work to do, but there is a well-defined focal point for decisions regarding the implementation of plans and procedures.

I learned the value of mailing lists during my first year of selling antiques. Some friends and I sent a post-card to all of the antique shops in New England. The postcard had attached to it a return postcard printed with our address. It stated that we would like to visit their shops and show them our "primitives" and folk art goods. If they returned the attached card, we knew that they were interested, and this response entitled them to a 10% discount on their first purchase with us.

By mailing those postcards, we learned which shops wanted us to visit. Some were not at all interested in our line. Others were somewhat curious but still purchased only to take advantage of the discount. As we went the full round of all the shops, we developed a list of the best buyers. Those special people became steady customers for many years. Less than 50 shops were on that list, but they purchased volumes of antiques. Throughout my business years, that list of dealers was the life-blood of my work and income. Occasionally, some owners died or retired. Others were added to the list at the suggestion of friends. The antique business was an excellent career that helped me to learn and to grow in many ways.

Now, I have found a correlation between my old work and my present vocation as a workshop presenter. When I first began my presentations, I asked every organization I could find to sponsor me. It worked. Then one year, on my birthday, I decided to adapt a postcard mailing for the workshops. I found a list of all the study groups for an organization to which I belonged, and I offered them each a gift on **my** birthday — a free copy of my current book! Most of the groups replied and were pleased with my book as an addition to their lending libraries. Later, I wrote to those respondents and offered to give a workshop for them. The responses were over-whelmingly positive; those study groups became my best sponsors.

Since that time, I have made the same offer to other organizations, and many have been added to my list. Many of those groups were very grateful that a well-known author and speaker could come to their community — often in remote rural areas. I felt honored by the hearty receptions I received.

Many people will want to hear **your** message. When creating your speaking schedule, strive to include new organizations, groups, and locations. Those groups also want new viewpoints — they will welcome the challenge to grow and to expand their understanding. It is nice to speak to the same audiences every year, but one should always be open to new opportunities. Some organizations have a high turn-over among their members, while others are slow to change. I'm pleased that my audiences are made-up of about 90% new faces. This tells me that I am reaching an ever-expanding group of people.

Because I now have a large list of "regulars" and "potentials" from which to draw, I try to encompass all of those areas when arranging my annual schedule. As with my file-card listing of antique shops, I go through the entire list by location, and then start over again with the first area. This procedure helps to even out my year's activities and allows me to make travel more effective when scheduling engagements.

The "secret" to using mailing lists is to offer something valuable to prospective clients or sponsors which will interest them in your work. As an antique dealer, I offered them a discount on their first purchase; as a workshop leader, I offered a free book for the group's library. Be sure your mailing is not just a "give me" request —offer to give them something, also.

The lists change very little over time, so they are easy to maintain. Those lists are **not** a general mailing list for people who have attended my programs or purchased my books by mail; rather they are special **lists of sponsors** that provide the life-stream for the body of my work.

Selling Products — Your Second Profit Center

Professional speakers often earn as much money through product sales as they will from an engagement commission or honorarium. As an antique dealer, I learned many valuable lessons in marketing products. First, appearance is very important. Your sale items must look good and be well packaged. Second, they must be priced appropriately to the value of your customer's need or desire.

You will sell books and tapes at your programs if they are readily available. People enjoy the convenience of obtaining your items on the spot, without having to wait for future delivery or having to pay shipping charges. The items must be on hand for workshop participants to purchase while their interest is at its peak. We all prefer immediate gratification when we have a strong urge to buy a product. Interest in a purchase decreases rapidly when there is a long wait to receive the satisfaction of delivery or if there are expensive shipping costs.

If you offer catalog or mail-order products, only a small percentage of your audience will order them from you. The public might genuinely want your items, but many people do not even keep extra stamps at home with which to mail the order form! Somehow, they just don't get around to ordering. They lose interest, and you lose the sale. If you must supply your items through the mail, encourage individuals to fill out order forms at your presentation and give them a reasonable estimate for delivery. You can often strengthen the **incentive** to order and to pay in advance at the presentation by offering free shipping if the order is placed during the workshop.

Throughout your presentation, give your audience the information they came to receive. Let them see your human side and have fun sharing with them. Be of service and value to them, and then — and only then — give a short "advertisement" near the close of your presentation. By the end of the day, your audience will have used several "break times" to browse through the products that are available. Most people will appreciate your explanation of materials that might be meaningful to them, personally.

A Hard Sell is No-Sell

Remember, the big secret of selling is to **relax**. Never appear to "push" for sales. Everyone knows that you would like to sell your items, but people feel uncomfortable if you have a hard sell approach. The hard-sell is out! People dislike high-powered sales, and many will refuse to buy simply because of any pressure tactics. They are fearful of spending good money based on "hype." They want to be convinced of the product's value. It is much more effective and profitable to replace the hard-sell pressure tactic that "you must buy today for a one-time-only opportunity or discount," with other incentives, such as the offer to autograph the books after the workshop. It has been my experience that individuals will purchase only the items they really want. Let them buy without pressure and enjoy watching the dynamic process of individuals finding that specific book or gift item.

Do not push for big sales, but be pro-active. Be prepared to demonstrate, to explain, or to answer questions related to your products. People expect you to be knowledgeable. It is important to know your products — their advantages and disadvantages.

It would be helpful for you to clarify your product-selling goals. List them in your journal or notebook so that you can refer to them. Ask yourself several questions about your goals for selling the products:

1. How much profit do I need to make from the sales? Do an analysis and assessment of your costs to produce the product and the percentage of income that you need to derive form the product sales.

2. Would I purchase the products at similar prices? Assess type and quality of material, the packaging, and the need that they will fill.

3. Do I enjoy making fine products available to people who will benefit from them? If so, what type of item do I most enjoy producing?

4. How do I feel about the work necessary to organize product sales?

There are many more questions to consider, both for yourself and for your customers. Seek feedback from your customers through verbal or written responses. What did they like? What was the most and least beneficial? How did they feel about the price and quality? What additional material would they like included?

When purchasing your sale merchandise, develop a good relationship with your vendors. Strive to get as good a deal as possible while maintaining quality and appearance. Sell for a fair price and forget trying to make excess profit. Over time, even a moderate amount of gain will add up, and you will be respected by your customers for maintaining high quality at a fair price.

Here are my own guidelines for product sales (but, of course, you might wish to create your own). During my presentation, I:

- keep the "commercial" between five and ten minutes in length.
- make it entertaining, adding a light bit of humor.
- hold up each book or tape for visual recognition and give a brief description.
- call attention to the price when something is an especially good buy; otherwise the price is clearly marked on each item.
- politely suggest that if people cannot afford an item, they may ask their library to purchase it. Sometimes study groups will purchase items to share together, thus saving money.
- give that short "commercial" near the end of the day and avoid referring to the sale products otherwise.

Remember, the "secret of sales" is to let people buy what they want. They will buy more than you could ever try to **sell** them. Demonstrate your goods, answer any questions, then stand back and be quiet!

The Big Question —
How to Set Your Speaking Fees

Throughout the two decades in which I have given programs, I have found that the question of fees varies widely. There are groups that expect a speaker to travel and give a program for free. There are others who will pay only a flat-rate, and when they say "flat", it usually **is** flat! Fortunately some sponsors are bountiful, and some facilitators are very generous.

Workshops are an excellent fund-raiser (and fun-raiser) for any organization. I believe that everyone should profit equally. After many years of giving workshops, I have created a payment plan that is designed specifically for one speaker giving a full-day program or workshop. The income of an event is from tuition or an attendance fee. **All** of the expenses are paid from the total attendance income. Expenses include the cost of mailing, the conference center or hotel meeting room, the speaker's travel costs (meals, lodging, transportation), and printing charges for program brochures or handouts. When all expenses are paid, the speaker and the organization divide the remaining profit **equally** — each receiving 50%. By this method, both do fair if the attendance is fair, well if the attendance is good, and great if the attendance is excellent. Both parties gain (or lose) in the same proportion. A simple formula would be:

1. Total income from attendance   _____.
2. Pay sponsors expenses   _____.
3. Pay speakers expenses   _____.
4. Equally divide remaining profit   _____.

Some speakers demand a minimum fee, but I feel this is unjust. Some organizations set a limit on how much the speaker can make, but this is just as unfair. Some programs lose money, some are marginal, some are good, and some are excellent. I believe the 50/50 system is the best for everyone. There is another option. Some facilitators allow the presenter to keep all the profits after expenses. Those are the generous souls that Kahlil Gibran called "believers in life and the bounty of life."

While the collection of payment is usually immediate and uncomplicated, there could be times when a speaker is not paid. Fortunately, such problems are rare — but I have experienced it. On one occasion, after I presented a workshop, the facilitator took all of the money and skipped town. She took both the expense money **and** the profits, and lost it all at a casino.

You might have programs that lose money, or barely break even. There also might be programs that do exceptionally well. If you analyze only one or two of your workshops, you will have a limited perspective, especially concerning finances. Some programs are winners financially and some are losers. It is best to consider the average income over several workshops to determine your true profit.

The same applies to your product expenses. It will require an up-front dollar investment and effort to gather all the materials and to generate the products you will sell. The amount averaged over a year's time will provide a more balanced statement of what is actually happening.

Your Advertising Budget

Your advertising costs can "make or break" your program. If you expect a positive outcome, you must allocate funds for advertising. Unless the right potential clients know of your workshop, the best presentation in the world might play to an empty room. When you plant seeds in a garden, you reap a harvest. If you plant nothing, you will reap nothing — except maybe weeds. The key is what, when, and where to plant. Ask yourself several questions to delineate your advertising goals. For instance: Who is the intended audience? How can I contact to this specific group?

If your topic is gardening, you would reach out to people near you who have purchased garden supplies or implements. The topic and the target audience determine the direction of outreach. Because the topic of gardening is so big, and the potential market is so general, you might consider a paid advertisement in a local paper or shoppers' news.

A more specific topic could be a special training course for nurse's aides. This market group is very limited and specific. You could gather a list of all such nurse's aides from a medical reference or a local hospital. Probably, there is a local or national association where you could access current mailing lists. You could purchase a mailing list from one of many commercial mailing list companies. General newspaper ads may not be as effective as a listing or notice in a health-related journal or newsletter. Commercial ads can be very expensive.

When a program is sponsored by an organization, that body, generally, is responsible for the advertising, and usually, very inexpensively can notify the target audience through regular newsletters and member publications. The organization does the planting for you but sometimes takes a substantial part of the harvest.

When and How to Plant

Sometimes a presenter will invest only a few dollars and attendance will be sizeable. Other times, the best seeds will be planted at the right time, and the harvest will be meager. There are many variables involved, both pro and con, such as word-of-mouth referrals; inclement weather on the day of the event; a conflicting TV program; a conflicting family activity or sporting event or coincidental adverse or positive publicity about the individual presenter, organization, or topic. There is no guaranteed formula for successful advertising, and it is difficult to know just when and where to advertise.

Keep in mind that an early mailing, flyers, and newsletters will inform people of the program's date and topic. A more specific and detailed reminder mailed approximately one month prior to the program will work best.

Easy Money

Most people would like to win the lottery. Perhaps, they assume that if they could win, then life would be perfect. Maybe; maybe not. Statistics show that lottery winners often have other problems and struggles.

Many writers, speakers, and teachers would like to be famous celebrities. But in any endeavor, wise and steady steps will accomplish more than wishing for a sudden windfall. After all, the journey can be as rewarding as the destination.

You might write a best-selling book. You could become a world-famous speaker. Some people do reach a high level of success but seldom on the first try or without experiencing failure first. Many opportunities will come, but don't spend your time on unrealistic fantasies. Rather, use your time to improve your writing, to fine-tune your presentation skills, and to develop the best material that you can. Be important to your field, but not self-important in your attitude.

Remember, a good book can help many people and is an important accomplishment. A sincere, heartfelt speaker is an inspiration to many. Perfect your God-given gifts and apply your talents. Very few people are lottery winners. Most people work their daily jobs and earn regular incomes. This approach might not make headlines, but it is practical and realistic.

Secrets of Repeat Business

There are some organizations that request my service every year, but I prefer to allow some time to pass between programs — preferably about two years — for two reasons. First, this allows other speakers to be heard (variety is the spice of life). Second, my participants need time to assimilate their experience, just as a good meal needs time to digest before another is enjoyed. Time also provides an interval for fresh material to evolve. When I develop a new program, I send a flyer describing that workshop to my list of about 200 facilitators and study groups.

Occasionally, people write and tell me that they have attended four, five, or even more of my programs. They like my material and benefit from the sessions. Those people become my "good will ambassadors" and tell their friends about my work. In time, you will have a similar following of people who genuinely like your presentations and your material. Always keep an open door for them. Encourage participants to write, or to call if you prefer to communicate by phone. But a following does not come quickly to every speaker. There is a secret to success — repeat business.

In the beginning, the high expense of attracting an audience through publicity, advertising, mailings, and phone calls, combined with other expenses might seem to outweigh the financial gains of the program itself. As the participants become familiar with your dedication to, and the quality of, the work, they will return and bring others with them and your followers will multiply. As you achieve recognition, you will see bigger profit potential. For instance, phone and electric companies do not make big profits on each call that you make or each load of laundry that you wash. Day by day, month after month, year after year, the profits begin to multiply.

To convince people to return, give them more than they expected for the price they paid. Give, give, and then give some more. Giving is the secret of a great presentation **and** the secret to a happier life. When people attend a program and the speaker fails to deliver, everyone is cheated. Participants know that they received a poor deal, and the speaker also is aware of the failure.

Workshops Are a Gift

When you give more than expected, people are amazed. At first, some do not believe it; a few even distrust your generosity. But, in time, the wheat is separated from the chaff; the givers are separated from the takers. You may think, "Well, I will give generously to those who will pay top dollar to attend." This is not a giving attitude. In one of the greatest books ever written, *The Prophet*, Kahlil Gibran writes:

> You often say, "I would give only to the deserving." The trees in your orchard say not so, nor the flocks on your pasture. They give that they may live, for to withhold is to perish.
> — Kahlil Gibran, *The Prophet*

Of giving, Gibran also writes:

> There are those who give little of the much which they have — and they give it for recognition — and their hidden desire makes their gifts unwholesome.
>
> And there are those who have little and give it all. These are the believers in life and the bounty of life, and their coffer is never empty.
>
> There are those who give with joy, and that joy is their reward.
>
> And there are those who give with pain, and that pain is their baptism.
>
> And there are those who give and know not pain in giving, nor do they seek joy, nor give with mindfulness of virtue;
>
> They give as in yonder valley the myrtle breathes its fragrance into space.
>
> — Kahlil Gibran, *The Prophet*

As a speaker and presenter, you will — above all — give of yourself. Your reward is a receptive and motivated audience. Workshops are a business — yes, but they also change lives. That is a compensation far greater than money!

Keep your priorities clear. Your income, most likely, will grow in direct proportion to the energy which you put into your work. Make your workshops work for people — give them valuable material and a profound experience. You will be rewarded!

What I Do That Works

1.   I start each workshop with a prayer. Many years ago, my own inner guidance advised me of the importance of this step. It's good for me, and especially

for any group with which I am working. My prayer is not from memory, or delivered by rote, but is an honest prayer for guidance and cooperation. I often am surprised by the verbal inspirations that come through me.

2. I make it clear that my workshop avoids the endless quandary involved in the discussion of various theories. Theory can clog the program. It can become bogged down in subsequent unfulfilling debate and conundrum. My approach to a workshop is purely practical: how can I help the participants to improve the quality of their lives — spiritually, physically, mentally, emotionally, or financially?

3. I employ guided sessions. People attend a workshop to do actual work upon a certain topic, and to experience the results. The more hands-on activities, the better, as long as the activities are relevant to the participants' growth and learning. Some people prefer the word *meditation;* others like the word *reverie;* some acknowledge the term, *self-hypnosis.* But for the sake of not offending anyone's favorite nomenclature, I now call my guided sessions, *Inner Adventures.* This term is inclusive and has a clear, positive focus.

4. I maintain humor. I was not always funny; in fact, I was so sour for so many years that people told me to practice smiling in a mirror! That is the truth, and I admit it. I was a bitter, angry person before I began using self-hypnosis as self-therapy. Self-hypnosis works. That is why I teach it! I even wrote a book about making self-hypnosis, positive programming tapes — tapes that people can make for themselves by reading aloud tested scripts into their own cassette recorders. Self-hypnosis is a life improvement tool.

A favorite excerpt from that book is entitled "Developing a Sense of Humor." I tested the sessions

for five years before the book's publication. I
employed the humor self-hypnosis sessions for a few
weeks, and I actually began to laugh. I found joy in
life. I began to joke more and to enjoy life immensely.
My wife, at that time, became concerned that I was
taking humor to an extreme. She insisted that I stop
using that particular tape. I did. Needless to say, we
are not together now. She's gone, but my sense of
humor remains.

When speaking, I occasionally use prepared jokes,
but humor (the real thing) just seems to come out. I like
it, and the audience appreciates a little levity —
especially when a workshop deals with powerful and
intense material. Humor balances deep subject matter
and affirms our humanity.

5. I allow people to tape-record a presentation.
This shows that I am not hiding anything and that
I am proud of and confident in my speech. The
tapes can continue to teach and to reach out to others,
even those who were unable to attend. Speaking
from a business point of view, if everyone went
home and shared the tape, the future audiences would
be forming.

What I Do That Does NOT Work

1. I lose a great deal of potential income by choosing
not to book appointments with individuals, while
holding a workshop or program. Some people become
very upset by this refusal, because they want to
experience a private session with the "big name"
speaker. I feel that when I (or any speaker) accept private
therapeutic sessions in proximity to a workshop
schedule, the main source of income then becomes the

appointments, and the workshop itself suffers. Therapists can appear to be "hustling" for private sessions (because they are lucrative), and this practice, I believe, is unbecoming and injurious to my field, but certainly not to all fields.

Worst of all, in this situation, the individual suffers. When a speaker comes to town, it often is a one-time event (or at most biennial), and so, the person in actual need of assistance has no follow-up for therapeutic help — the "big name" is in some other city.

I encourage workshop participants who want therapy to "follow up" their attendance at my presentation with visits to a **local** therapist or healer. In fact, time permitting, I encourage any local healers and health-care professionals in the audience to come up and to speak briefly about their areas of expertise. This information can be most enlightening; many people are simply not aware of the many gifted healers residing in their own area.

2. Signing autographs during the working day is simply too hard to do while trying to find time to make a trip to the bathroom! I have found that asking the audience to wait until the end of the program before requesting autographs works much better. I have discovered that I am a better speaker if I also am permitted to indulge in the "pause that refreshes". Speakers are human, too!

Props, Slides, Overheads

A blackboard, whiteboard, or flip chart provides the means to sketch or to illustrate a point. Such props can be used in various ways. I prefer the dry-erase whiteboard, which can be erased cleanly and easily.

What I do NOT suggest is the use of slides or overhead projector transparencies. They often seem to malfunction. Also, with the lights dim, your audience will tend to become sleepy. Unless you are giving a talk on birds, for example, and absolutely need slides of birds, I would recommend not using them! Find some other means of illustrating your program.

The purpose and design of your program are the significant features; props are used for enhancement. Our local library sponsors a young man who visits the library with a van full of live snakes — in cages, of course! His purpose is to teach about and to demonstrate the value of snakes, how to differentiate the non-poisonous from the poisonous types, and to teach respect for all of God's creatures.

One would think that this program would be shunned because most people tend to fear snakes. Each year, people come from all around to attend his presentation. The man begins with an introduction to snakes, handling them at the same time. He explains that later the audience (including many children) will be allowed to touch them. The children grimace or shake their heads as if to say, "No Way!" But, in less than an hour, just about everybody is handling the snakes, and several people are volunteering to line up and to support a giant python as it stretches out, cradled by pairs and pairs of excited, willing, little hands.

The presenter knows his topic, he respects his props, and he conveys a message of safety and wisdom to which his audience responds. It is always a treat to participate in such an educational program. When you teach what you love — as that speaker does — the audience will love you also.

Let People Know

When you become known for your outreach work, let people know when and where you will be speaking. Print your schedule for the upcoming year. The secret here is to have booked as many engagements as possible. A full calendar looks much better than a sparse one.

As you become increasingly visible, more people and organizations will become interested in your work. Success generates success. As you become increasingly active and popular as a speaker, you will be in demand!

Self-Evaluation for Self-Improvement

A good method for improving your presentation is reading the participants' evaluation forms after the program. Usually such forms are handed out by a sponsoring organization and are helpful to read.

A better method of self-analysis is to tape record your program. Then, after a few days, listen to your taped presentation. This has taught me how to improve my work! As I did, you will become aware of specific areas that need improvement.

Perhaps the best method of self-improvement is your own video tape; you can hear yourself speaking and can see your gestures — your TOTAL stage presence. Study the video and ask friends to comment on your delivery, mannerisms, and so forth. When I watch a video of my performance, it is very humbling — but, it's most effective in helping me to improve my work.

You do not need expensive video equipment to film your program. Ask a friend to lend you a home video

Program Schedule for Henry Leo Bolduc
P.O. Box 88, Independence, VA 24348 USA

January
Virginia Beach, Virginia
January 27, Saturday
LIFE PATTERNS, SOUL LESSONS
& FORGIVENESS
Workshop
Contact: A.R.E. Registrar 1-800-333-4499

February
Bristol, Tennessee
February 10, Saturday
*THE 4TH DIMENSION
Workshop
Contact: Ruby Gillion (615) 764-3940

Mercedes, Texas
February 24, Saturday
LIFE PATTERNS, SOUL LESSONS
& FORGIVENESS
Workshop
Contact: Bobbi Jones (210) 565-1035

March
Pittsburgh, Pennsylvania
March 9, Saturday
LIFE PATTERNS, SOUL LESSONS
& FORGIVENESS
Workshop
Contact: Dr. Edward Stegman (412) 963-1144

Winnipeg, Manitoba, Canada
March 23, Saturday
LIFE PATTERNS, SOUL LESSONS
& FORGIVENESS
Workshop
Contact: Marjorie Reynolds (204) 452-1035

Winnipeg, Manitoba, Canada
March 24, Sunday
Advanced Professional Training
Special Class
Contact: Marjorie Reynolds (204) 452-1035

Seabeck, Washington
March 29, 30, 31
LIFE PATTERNS, SOUL LESSONS
& FORGIVENESS
3-Day Retreat
Contact: Shirley Anne Schaudies
(206) 943-7069 or 943-2512

April
Sedona/Verde Valley, Arizona
April 27, Saturday
*THE 4TH DIMENSION
Workshop
Contact: Lee Leffel (520) 634-0408 or Joan
Lambard (520) 298-0759

April *continued*
Tucson, Arizona
April 28, Sunday
*THE 4TH DIMENSION
Workshop
Contact: Virginia Hollond (602) 298-0759

May
Washington, D.C.
May 2, 3, 4, 5
ASSOCIATION FOR PAST-LIFE
RESEARCH & THERAPY
Conference
A major event for professionals and the general
public. Henry will give a Pre-Conference
Institute May 2.
Contact: A.P.R.T. (909) 784-1570

Albany, New York
May 11, Saturday
*THE 4TH DIMENSION
Workshop
Contact: Paula Hungerford (203) 264-7906

Hartford, Connecticut
May 12, Sunday
*THE 4TH DIMENSION
Workshop
Contact: Paula Hungerford (203) 264-7906

Falls Church, Virginia
May 18, Saturday
*THE 4TH DIMENSION
Workshop
Contact: Julius Hankin (703) 734-1024

June
Wytheville, Virginia
June 15, Saturday
THE JOURNEY WITHIN
Workshop
Contact: Henry or Joan (540) 655-4523

Virginia Beach, Virginia
June 17, Monday
ONENESS THROUGH APPLICATION
A.R.E. Congress Week
Contact: 1-800-333-4499

Dublin, Ireland
June 29, Saturday
HYPNOSIS — CREATING YOUR
OWN DESTINY
Workshop
Contact: Irish School of Ethical & Analytical
Hypnotherapy, Tuckey Hours, 8 Tuckey St.,
Cork City, Ireland

This is an example of a year's progam schedule.

June *continued*

Dublin, Ireland
June 30, Sunday
HEALING THE PAST —
BUILDING THE FUTURE
Workshop
Contact: Joe E. Keaney, Tuckey Hours, 8 Tuckey
St., Cork City, Ireland 021-273575

July

Lintgen, Luxembourg
July 6, Saturday
HEALING THE PAST —
BUILDING THE FUTURE
Workshop
Contact: Franz Bondy 352 328850

Lintgen, Luxembourg
July 7, Sunday
LIFE PATTERNS, SOUL LESSONS
& FORGIVENESS
Workshop
Contact: Franz Bondy 352 328850

Paris, France
July 13, Saturday
THE JOURNEY WITHIN
Workshop
Contact: Rene and Estrella Pellin (1) 34 21 56 31

Paris, France
July 14, Sunday
LIFE PATTERNS, SOUL LESSONS
& FORGIVENESS
Workshop
Contact: Rene and Estrella Pellin (1) 34 21 56 31

San Francisco Bay Area
July 27, Saturday
HEALING THE PAST —
BUILDING THE FUTURE
Workshop
Contact: Grethe Tedrick (510) 234-0415

August

Nashua, New Hampshire
August 8-11, Thursday-Saturday
NATIONAL GUILD OF HYPNOTISTS
CONVENTION
Henry will present various talks and
workshops throughout the convention. This
annual convention is open to the general public
as well as to professionals. The best in the
world! On August 8th, Henry will present a
full-day Summer Institute.
Contact: National Guild (603) 429-9438

October

Columbus, Ohio
October 5, Saturday
*THE 4TH DIMENSION
Workshop
Contact: Marti Coblentz (614) 457-8034

Findlay, Ohio
October 6, Sunday
*THE 4TH DIMENSION
Workshop
Contact: Emory Michaels (419) 394-7865

Morgantown/Reading, Pennsylvania
October 12, Saturday
*THE 4TH DIMENSION
Workshop
Contact: Marsha Graft (610) 926-4485

November

Charlottesville, Virginia
November 2, Saturday
LIFE PATTERNS, SOUL LESSONS
& FORGIVENESS
Workshop
Contact: QUEST INSTITUTE 1-800-346-9223

Charleston, West Virginia
November 9, Saturday
*THE 4TH DIMENSION
Workshop
Contact: Rich Hopkins (304) 746-7700

Houston, Texas
November 16, Saturday
*THE 4TH DIMENSION
Workshop
Contact: Joe Steelman (713) 893-4540

December

Wytheville, Virginia
December 2-7
PAST LIFE THERAPY TRAINING INTENSIVE
Certificate Course for Counselors, Health-Care
Professionals, Therapists and Past-Life
Researchers. Write for more information to:
Intensive Training Program, P.O. Box 88,
Independence, VA 24348, USA

NOTE: ALL 4th Dimension workshops are
given by BOTH Henry Bolduc and Henry
Reed; the 2-Henrys.

IMPORTANT NOTE: *We are presently
scheduling for our 1997 Workshops. If you
would like one of Henry Leo's programs in
YOUR area, call (540) 655-4523.*

recorder. While filming, remember to address your audience, not the video camera. Save the tape. In later years, you will be amazed at how much you have improved your delivery.

Evaluations: On a Scale of One to Ten ...

One way an audience evaluates a speaker, which also can supply feedback, is by means of evaluation forms. Such completed forms are important, because they help the speaker to improve his or her performance. A friend wrote to me concerning a speaker who had presented a weekend program in his area.

The particular speaker was well-known (had appeared on television) and was assumed to be a competent presenter. "Although the subject matter was interesting, the weekend was a dry and disappointing experience for the audience," he wrote. Take note of this presenter's failure and avoid the mistakes he made.

The speaker did not follow the printed time schedule for the program and did not initiate breaks. Set a specific time for taking breaks and announce them before you begin speaking, so that people can anticipate when they will be able to use the restroom or otherwise refresh themselves. Surely, the presenter must have noticed that people were leaving in the middle of the program to take their own breaks. Personally, I don't like to miss any part of a program that I am attending, and I'm sure that others feel the same.

My friend reported that there was almost no group interaction. People simply "sat" for the entire weekend. Individuals attend workshops not only for the lecture but to meet other people. Some people are seeking to meet others of like mind, but need an extra boost to do so. In this respect, a presenter's encouragement that they link up with others at lunch or during free time to discuss the experiences is a worthwhile suggestion that can make a difference.

Another flaw in the presenter's performance was the misuse of the meditation experience which — according to my correspondent — rendered it practically ineffective. The background music was so scratchy, distorted, and loud, that one could hardly hear the presentation. Apparently, the meditation was rushed by talking "a mile a minute." To further complicate a bad situation, there was only partial use of the microphone both during the meditation and the lecture.

While years of experience can teach what works and what doesn't work in the context of a presentation, many people often are unaware of all the little things that dramatically affect the outcome of a program. That speaker had excellent academic knowledge but limited "speaking skills" for working with groups.

Of course, there were some good comments concerning that weekend. It is always wiser and more balanced to evaluate equally both the positive and the negative aspects of any experience. To go one step further, perhaps it is **better** to focus more upon the good than the bad. A fault can be over-emphasized until perspective is lost, or some things that occur are not even be the fault of the speaker at all.

Apparently insignificant points can make the difference when setting the tone for a workshop. For instance, should the registrar be late and lines of people are waiting impatiently, the day begins poorly and everyone is inclined to be critical and unhappy. I have noticed that when the registrar is on time, it sets the correct pace for the entire day. This is such a simple thing, **but so important!** Early arrivals can receive their workshop manuals and begin reading them, which is an excellent preparation for the upcoming event. Long lines do not form at the door, and a sense of calm and order prevails.

Personal Satisfaction

While many aspects of my work are pleasing to me, there are three that give me special happiness. First, each autumn is the time when I compile my speaking and workshop schedule for the upcoming year. There is great pleasure in anticipating the year to come, and I carefully plan specific destinations with both outreach and adventure in mind.

Second, simply being an author has many rewards, although in my field they tend to be manifested more often in spiritual rather than in financial form. Something happened very recently that has affected me deeply. Often, people will say that they have read one of my books, and their comments concerning it might be quite complimentary. Perhaps an author grows to expect — even while appreciating — such comments.

When a man stopped me at a large convention and made a point of saying that he had read ALL of my books, I realized that there is very clear distinction between simply reading a book and actually being a **student** of a particular writer's discipline. Although at the time, I failed to be fully aware of this man's comment. I now realize and truly appreciate his obvious dedication to my subject. This experience was both humbling and exalting.

Third, as a presenter I always ask those in attendance to write directly to me if they have more questions, or if they desire free source materials concerning anything that I discussed during the workshop. I answer the letters, and I appreciate this continuing connection with my audiences. Sometimes, life-long friendships are formed by such correspondence.

Some might think that it is a burden to answer every letter. I believe it to be a great honor. I sincerely appreciate the hundreds of letters that I receive annually, and I keep them organized in a large cabinet. Those letters — besides their obviously heart-warming value — also tell me which topics are of current interest to those who might come to future workshops.

Another bonus related to presenting workshops is the letters of gratitude which a speaker receives. People will respond to your outreach, and they will write to thank you.

Artist: Kathye Mendes

Write with reason — speak with passion.

At first, you might be embarrassed by those letters of praise. Remember, it is honest praise. Audiences will thank you. Some will even say which item or topic helped them the most. It seems amazing, but people will be given the exact material that they need and want. Their thanks is simply another "perk" for a job well done. Be grateful for such letters and words of appreciation.

Chapter Seven
Travel and Workshops

Getting it Together

One good reason to give workshops is to have opportunities for travel! I love to go just about anywhere and everywhere. If people will listen, I will go to speak! As a professional speaker whose business is giving workshops, a number of my travel expenses are tax deductible. Any speaker must check with an accountant or financial advisor as to what rules apply. A part-time speaker or writer also is allowed many deductions and benefits.

Often my programs take me overseas. (My previous career in the antiques business also took me to many foreign lands.) It might seem obvious, but in the process of travel, people meet other travelers, those who have learned the secret of travel. The **secret** of traveling? Yes!

The "secret" of distant travel involves three things:
1. A passport or other travel documents
2. Money or another medium of exchange (credit cards, traveler's checks, etc.)
3. The desire to go

Which is the most important? I would choose number three: **the desire to travel.** Passports are easy to obtain. It costs about 10 cents a week to own a passport. Many people have the money to travel, but the DESIRE to travel is the one necessary, yet intangible quality. Either you have the spirit of discovery and adventure, or you don't. You love to travel and to experience life in new ways — or you don't. Desire can lead you to whatever you really want in life!

Life on the Road — Foreign and Domestic

Everyone's life has milestones. For some, accomplishment is measured by financial savings or material acquisitions. For others, success is measured by an elegant home or high performance vehicles. Others revel in business promotions, or academic degrees. I, however, measure the success of my life by travel passports!

I am now filling my sixth passport! This is both my personal success story and the status symbol of a dedicated traveler. My parents are of French-Canadian heritage, and we traveled frequently to Canada in my youth. Later, in my teens, I began traveling to other countries and then to other continents. I have learned that there is an art and a science to travel.

Much of what I know about travel comes, of course, by actual experience. It is difficult to learn about traveling from a book and much of the information might not be current. Fellow travelers are often a much more helpful source of updated information. Years of practical experience have taught me to apply what I know about traveling to the presentation of workshops.

It is quite likely that, once you have become proficient in giving workshops in your own country, your next step will be to reach out and to present programs in foreign nations. This is an exciting opportunity for any speaker! People of other lands are **very** appreciative when a speaker is willing to travel thousands of miles to bring them a valuable experience.

It is crucial to select the proper luggage for your travels. Airlines allow two pieces of luggage, but there are few requirements as to size; luggage weight is hardly a factor now (if kept within reason). I have found that it is very important to pack workshop materials, manuals, **and** items for sale — even if your audience is **not** English speaking. Books and manuals are quite heavy, so buy sturdy suitcases.

My two suitcases have served me well for many years. They are made of heavy duty plastic and have wheels, as well as handles for pulling. The larger the wheels, the better the stability. Appearance is unimportant; just make certain that your luggage is strong and durable. There is no reason to spend extra money on appearance since your luggage will immediately begin to show wear (scratches, stains, etc.) from the rough handling it will receive when loaded on airplanes, trains, etc.

Relatively few companies manufacture luggage, and consequently, many pieces look alike. This can be a problem, and many people have lost luggage because of this fact. Mark your luggage so that you can spot it from a distance. Name tags are often torn off in handling, so do not depend on them. Define your luggage in bold and obvious ways, and you will save yourself the possibility of many losses and delays. For convenience, purchase luggage with built-in combination locks which provide easy access and security without the nuisance of keys.

It will be necessary to assemble a practical travel wardrobe. For me, clothing is not a priority. Books, tapes, and manuals **are.** When selecting clothing, pack everyday items that you currently wear, not new clothes — and especially not new shoes! Since ironing is not easy when you are on the road, buy wrinkle-free materials. If you are invited to stay with a local sponsor or facilitator, arrangements can usually be made for your laundry. Many foreign countries now have laundromats — a convenience that was unavailable until a few years ago.

Free Travel — A Gift of Great Value

As you begin to travel, whether frequently or occasionally, be sure to obtain a Frequent Traveler card from the airline(s) that you use most. PLEASE enter this program even if you do not fly often. It pays. First of all, the program is absolutely free to join, and there is almost no paperwork involved. The airline does it all for you. All you have to do is give your "frequent traveler number" whenever you check in for a flight or when you purchase your tickets.

The benefits are enormous! You may redeem your free points for airline tickets or a complete tour package. I have applied my points toward a number of flights, both for myself and for my family. If you are not already a frequent flyer, you are by default, a frequent loser in terms of dollars and cents.

Best of all, I now can accumulate mileage points with my American Express card. I use my card both at home and abroad, and I put most business expenses on that card. The points add up quickly! I dream of exotic vacations ... (some day, when I actually retire).

Fortune continues to yield amazing bonuses. Now, since I receive even more mileage points when I use the telephone, long-distance calls are no longer a source of guilt! Even some grocery stores give mileage points! Life gives us so many blessings!

How to Have Great Vacations
Just About Anywhere — For Free

The way to experience a "free" vacation is to combine work with pleasure. Go a few days early, or stay over at your destination some extra days, and utilize this opportunity to enjoy some relaxation.

Doctors, lawyers, and most other professionals seldom hold conferences or training seminars in dull, uninspiring places. THEY know the value of combining business affairs with exotic locations. In fact, some so-called seminars are actually vacations **disguised** as business trips! But this is NOT what I am suggesting to you. I AM suggesting that you set aside a little extra time during your legitimate speaking tour to include visiting friends or family, or a bit of rest and relaxation.

This "R and R" will also improve your performance as a speaker. Audiences can tell when a speaker has just arrived in town and rushed to a seminar. There is a certain bedraggled appearance of jet lag. Go early, take time to have fun, and your journey as a speaker — as well as your journey through life — will be the better for it.

If you have always wanted to go to another country, a speaking engagement is a great way to get you there! Connect with corporations or organizations that have international networks. Cooperate with them by giving training or motivational programs at their foreign locations.

Some presenters work with certified travel organizations which sponsor oceanic cruises or tours to foreign countries. In this case, the speaker travels for free.

Last but not least, if you have contacts in other lands, ask those people to facilitate your program. Once a few programs have been given in other countries, you will see how easy it is. Apply what you've learned at home toward the success of your speaking engagements abroad. Basically, the same techniques work anywhere in the world. If you like to travel, you'll be able to go virtually anywhere in the world and **make** money. A good speaker can cover all the expenses of travel and even make a profit.

Translating Workshops into Other Languages

Because of my love for travel, I have worked with numerous translators. The translator **hears** words in one language and **repeats** those words in another language. Although there are professional translators who are meticulous and scholarly, my choice is with informal translators. (Technically, **translations** are usually of the written word — the translation of a book, for instance. Interpretations are of the **spoken** word; a speech is interpreted. None the less, I prefer the word "translation" in both cases, because "interpretation" has an implication of adulterating the original meaning.)

Often, when I present a workshop in another country, most of the people there do not speak English. A translator is necessary. Although I am able to speak in several languages, a translator can present sophisticated concepts and terminology more proficiently.

Initially, when presenting programs for translation, I assumed that the extra time needed for interpretation would lessen the amount of required material. I was wrong. I spoke only a few sentences or a paragraph, then the translator immediately repeated that material in the language of the audience. There was virtually no time lapse. The translator is quiet while I say a few sentences, then I am quiet during the translation when I plan my next few sentences, making them as clear and suscinct as possible.

In every foreign audience, there are individuals who speak English very well. Sometimes the translator is provided a more appropriate word or phrase by some-one in the audience. Such "coaching" is fun, and the audience enjoys the spontaneity of "live" informal translations. Participants reveal their own insights into my material by assisting the translator.

Yes, you can go anywhere in the **world** and present your programs. Language need not be a barrier. Having worked with a translator has made me a better speaker, and it has brought new perspectives to people who would otherwise have had no access to it.

Travel Can Be "Upsetting"

It is my hope that this book will give you VALUABLE information and procedures which I employ in the areas of writing, speaking, and giving workshops. Ironically, in order to do this task fully, I must discuss a subject that many people find offensive, but of which they should be aware. If the topic of hu-man body functions is offensive to you, please skip the next three paragraphs.

Advertisements politely call it "irregularity," but it is really constipation. This inconvenience can ruin any workshop leader. Anyone who sits at a desk for long hours is aware of this problem. Speakers who travel and catch fast food meals "on the run" are very vulnerable to this problem. Workshop presenters who frequently cross time zones during travel to other countries are likely to encounter this difficulty.

The symptoms are clear — at least to others: sluggishness, irritability, lack of humor, bad breath, etc. The solution is simple, and it can save you both physical and social anguish. Fig bars. That's it! It's that simple and effective. Forget the pills and medications; some are dangerous and unpredictable. Fig bars — THE great secret. (Remember who gave you this valuable advice!) Incidentally, don't believe the TV ads that tell you to take breath mints to "cover up" the problem. In most cases "mints" deal only with the effect, not the cause.

The opposite extreme can be troublesome, also. For some, any traveling —especially to other countries — can bring on diarrhea which is often caused by the local water. To avoid the situation, buy and use bottled water — even for rinsing your tooth brush. Take care, also, to avoid local ice cubes and salads which have been prepared by using water from the faucet.

When a problem does occur, natural remedies are better than synthetic. If you find yourself in this situation, eat dry crackers, plain bread, or cheese. Eat healthy foods to avoid problems; you will be happier, healthier, and of better service to others.

Another valuable tip to avoid an upset is to pay close attention to the restaurants you patronize. Often, the cleanliness of the bathroom is an indication of the cleanliness of the kitchen!

What Price Fashion?

In balance to my enthusiasm for travel, I must remind you to avoid the "Law of Agony", meaning to be careful and wise in your journeying. Leave the expensive and glittering jewelry safely at home. Dress for adventure, not for glamour. Do not be pretentious, for you could attract the opposite of what you intended. Always be careful, but avoid being paranoid. Pack plenty of practical common-sense into your travel bags. Display your kindness and social graces. Dress for comfort; don't be a victim of fashion.

Here is a tip that can save you money, and at the same time, will allow you to contribute to the local economy of poorer countries. Take clothing that you do not particularly like or do not wear too often. Then, as you finish wearing it, leave it behind. Someone will claim it. Tell the maid at your hotel that you are discarding it, or place it in the trash to make it clear that you don't want the items. This method will save on costly laundry bills, will help someone else in need who will "inherit" your clothing, and will make room in your suitcases for more valuable items on the return trip. Every country has items you can purchase to bring home, and you deserve to return with treats and treasures rather than dirty laundry.

I'm not suggesting that you travel the world munching on fig bars and leaving a trail of dirty laundry behind you. I am suggesting that you do everything possible to make your journey safe, easy, and trouble-free. Travel is difficult enough without adding to problems that will arise naturally. Learn to give yourself lots of treats. Be easy with yourself, your travel companions, and the people you visit.

Artist: Kathye Mendes

I'm not suggesting that you travel the world munching on fig bars and leaving a trail of dirty laundry behind you.

A Note for the Truly Adventurous

As a writer, speaker, or teacher, you can live in almost any country, town, or village on earth! It is possible that while presenting your workshops abroad, you will discover a location that is truly "home" to you. You can live just about anywhere you wish and travel to your engagements.

Any person who possesses initiative and a spirit of adventure will find it easy to relocate. If you have only a little money, you can find countries where the cost of living is low. There your money will stretch further, and you can live VERY well with very little. You can retire at a young age, rent a small home, and live comfortably on a modest income. If you have money, you can live very well in more affluent areas. You can buy or rent a nice place, enjoy a new land, and start a new life.

A Unity in Humanity

I am a big advocate of travel because it teaches many valuable lessons. Two main reasons to travel are to visit PLACES and to meet PEOPLE. "Places" are historical sites, holy shrines, temples, monuments, museums, natural wonders, etc. Those are worthy and important destinations. Meeting people is perhaps the greater reason because, by this means, we connect with all humanity. By traveling, you can become an unofficial Goodwill Ambassador. Every person who travels is an ambassador of his or her nation — for good or ill.

YES! Travel, to me, is the greatest teacher for humanity — and about humanity. We are connected by the very fact that we are on the planet together! We are all enrolled in this vast school called Earth.

People everywhere love their children just as we do. They breathe from the same atmosphere, are warmed from the same sun, and washed by the same rain. All people are equally our brothers and sisters at the spiritual level.

In their journeys, people connect with other people everywhere; they LIVE a shared humanity. They discover truths beyond what books can teach; they realize deeper meaning than the media portrays. They can embrace life everywhere, even among their seeming enemies. Opportunities for love and forgiveness come in abundance. If we love only those who love us, how have we grown?

Exploration

Be sure to wander the back roads of other countries. Don't fall into the routine of just visiting the major tourist sites. The everyday aspects of life are rich in meaning and discovery. Once, while in France, my wife and I drove down a dirt road to a tiny village. We spotted a cemetery and decided to tour it. There we witnessed a very amazing tombstone. A young man had died in a motorcycle accident and his family had requested that his tombstone be carved in an exact replica of his motorcycle! There was even a poem engraved on the stone, explaining how much the young man had loved his motorcycle and how it had eventually brought about his death. This is an example of the unusual and touching sites you will see if you take the time to depart from an established itinerary.

When Joan and I travel, we strive to be aware of local customs and ways of life. Most of all, we take time to talk to the local people and are often impressed with their wisdom and kindness.

Travel often is rushed, but we plan for rest and reflection from our busy pace. Sometimes, a city park is a prefect place, in populated areas, to sit and to observe daily life. Traveling requires such quiet times to balance the frenzy of activity.

When **you** have traveled, what were your favorite places? Your least favorite? Why? Where would you like to go on your next trip? What are the greatest lessons that travel has taught you? If you could pay for your trips by giving talks or seminars, **where** would you most like to speak? Pause and ponder the answers. Then, move straight ahead to become a well-seasoned traveler.

What is a Well-Seasoned Traveler?

"Well-seasoned" is an expression describing a person who is experienced in traveling or who travels well. For some, travel can be a challenge. The "secret" is the traveler's attitude and his or her willingness to adapt to changing environments and to different people.

Travel is both an art and a science. The "science" involves scheduling, currency exchanges, hotel accommodations, meals, etc. The "art" is making it all seem easy and fun; doing hard work in confidence and comfort. The science of travel can be learned from books; the art can be acquired only through experience. Some people seem to understand the mechanics of travel instinctively.

Travel connects you with the mainstream of life. It is the best teacher. Lessons learned while traveling can be of lasting value. Travel is about life — the giving, receiving, and sharing of experiences. I highly encourage self-directed, independent travel — whether you use travel for speaking and teaching classes or for pleasure.

By now, you must realize that I am a BIG advocate of all travel. I admit this wholeheartedly because it's true. I love to travel, and I hope that you will learn its value. I encourage you to travel and also to teach as you go. Let your inner wisdom guide you to the lands of your heart's memories. Most of all, travel for the **fun** of it. Experience life! Live the adventure!

The well-seasoned traveller.

Artist: Jeffrey Winchester

Chapter Eight
A Holistic Perspective

Complementary Learning

In working with the information and techniques in this book, you'll observe that some keywords are: travel, learn, and grow. In addition, discover, create, and experience are just as significant. Through the application of those six words, you could invent and design an exciting career that maximizes income and self-esteem.

Writing is the logical foundation for your speaking material. Speaking opens a channel of inspiration for writing. Good writing and clear speaking make for excellent teaching. The individual parts of your work will improve the whole. The concept, termed **holistic**, indicates the involvement of the whole person or the whole package.

In other words,
> Speaking helps writing
> Writing helps speaking
> Speaking and writing help teaching
> Teaching will help speaking and writing

A good book, like a good journey, always ends with a new beginning. This is YOUR beginning, YOUR call to adventure, YOUR invitation to action. NOW is the opportunity for your next step in your mission. There is an old axiom that states, "If you go looking for trouble, you probably will find it." There is truth in that saying, but its opposite also is true. In other words, if you go looking for adventure, you probably will find adventure. Whatever you truly seek — love, wisdom, service, or anything else — you, eventually, will find.

Your teachings could encourage and inspire thousands; your creative writings could help to enlighten millions. The number of people who could be reached — and helped — through your work and your gifts to humanity are unimaginable. This isn't meant to promote vanity or to foster self-importance, but it is a truth provided for you in a loving and advisory manner. Be kind. Be simple. There is great beauty in simplicity and true strength in gentleness.

Long-term Success

Although everyone likes attention and accolades, such rewards are not necessary for success. **Accomplishment** is what is important. True accomplishment is not always evident to the world, and the media does not always acknowledge your work. There are those who work hard for a lifetime on a project and are never recognized; others do just a little in a specific area and get great credit. Who knows why? Maybe it is good karma from other lives finally coming to them or, maybe, they are just well-connected with media/power brokers. Perhaps they are in the right place at the right time. But acknowledged or not, inner knowledge of success is lasting.

Many great men and women from the past were not fully recognized or appreciated in their own time for their accomplishments. Learn from this fact. Do not be

Your Creative Voice is Your Gift to Humanity

Artist: Sue Jones

overly-concerned if your work is not fully appreciated in your lifetime. If your contributions are of lasting value, they will be remembered. Relatively few individuals in every era become "rich and famous" while still alive. Maybe that will happen to you, but one thing is sure — unless you try, you'll never know. In other words, you can only reap the harvest after you have planted the seeds. No one can guarantee fame and fortune; but I can assure you that you will become a wiser person by whole-heartedly doing your work.

The good that we do is always recorded in the soul records. The harm that we do is also recorded. What might appear to be good in the eyes of the media might not always be so in spirit. What the media might fail to report could be of immense value to humanity. Just because something is popular or unpopular does not guarantee its true value. What you do and what you give to others is of the greatest value. Credit and applause are minor compared to the qualities of goodness and kindness — qualities that must be of your very essence.

Your truths — those you have discovered for yourself — have value and importance, and you not only have the right to share them, you have a responsibility to humanity. You will gain satisfaction in sharing your truth. The most secure and motivated people learn to live beside "the system" — not above it, not below it, just beside it. For "the system" (as it is called) is a political maze and an entrapment. Many people are caught up in it and use the social structure to gain power and to promote it above all else. Just remember, the wise person finds a suitable way of living in the world while remaining free of the world's snares and pitfalls.

We live in an amazing world. It is a place of action and response, of planting and reaping. It is evident that when we DO something, it gets done; similarly, if we fail to do something, it doesn't get done. It helps that the rules are so simple and clear. The same laws apply to you and to your work with writing, speaking, and presenting seminars/workshops. If you DO the steps involved, you will get the job accomplished.

The level of accomplishment you achieve is based exactly on your level of commitment and action. When you take the time to write, whether formally or informally, the words get on paper. When you speak to people, whether to one person or to a thousand, you are sharing ideas and information. When you organize a workshop or program, you group your thoughts, your talks, and your writings into a neat bundle. You tie it all together into a beautiful package which is your gift to humanity.

If you merely read this book and do not take action, you will have accomplished nothing lasting. If you read and think about doing, it is a little better, but you still are lacking the satisfaction of living what you have studied. If you read, decide to act, and then set in motion what you have studied, you are fulfilling the intent of this book. When you use your mind — guided by your spirit — to act, you are a builder, a creator of a better life and a better world.

Action - Reaction

When people notice that you are succeeding in your outreach work, some are pleased and will encourage you; others, sad to say, become jealous and act differently. Human nature is the same the world over. Wise people will help and encourage you; the mean-spirited, boorish ones work to undermine your efforts.

Oftentimes, the cynical ones will strike when you are most defenseless and vulnerable. A certain degree of intelligence is required to be a cynic, but to rise above the temptation of cynicism requires the higher level of wisdom and some emotional maturity.

So, what can you do about criticism? I think there are three possibilities. First, you can ignore it and deprive your critics of attention (Probably, they will focus on someone else). Ignoring is a form of denial, but it does work. The problem probably does not reside with you, anyway; critical, disdainful people actively search for their victims.

Secondly, you can resist your critics. You can answer their allegations and deny their charges. The problem with this approach is that you will waste valuable time and effort (and maybe, money) in defending yourself. Cynics, on the other hand, just keep up an endless barrage of criticism. This approach is likened to arguing with a drunk — you waste time, perhaps get into a fight, and the next day the drunk doesn't remember what the argument was all about.

The third approach is more subtle. It neither ignores the boors, nor does it rebut them. It is simply deciding to take the offensive instead. This approach is choosing to take action of **your** choice and direction. It is very different from what most people think of doing at first, but it is far more productive than most ever imagine.

For example, when I was in high school, the administration decided to impose a dress code which prohibited wearing jeans to class. A wise teacher suggested that rather than **reacting** to this new regulation, the students should **act** by wearing suits, white shirts, and ties. The students looked good, felt good, and got their point across without confrontation.

The dress code was dropped, and neither the students nor the administration lost.

No matter what you want to teach or to present, there will be someone, somewhere, who will criticize. Take that criticism lightly; don't react to it. No one can tell you how to approach each and every challenge or how to tackle every dilemma. The key is to study the situation and to find a solution that is neither reactionary nor denying in nature. It is far wiser to take the initiative — to move ahead with your own program. Concentrate on improving what you do; **your** agenda.

Discouragement is human and a part of life. The solution is to monitor and to regulate the low times and, then, to MAKE yourself get up and do something positive. Wisely, it has been said that instead of cursing the darkness, light candles. What can you do that is positive? Many things come to mind: write an article, a poem, a letter to a friend, speak to someone who will help you through the fog, help someone else who is having a difficult time, volunteer in the community, take a walk in nature, etc. Doing **something** is the key. You don't have to do everything in the world, but you can do something creative and productive.

Life requires effort; in turn, those efforts strengthen the fiber of life. Writing good crisp material is not always easy. Public speaking takes courage, but it also builds courage. Although great workshops require planning and hard work, the rewards are well worth the effort. It is especially fortunate if you are a pioneer in your field. Today's innovation can become tomorrow's tradition.

In Earth School, we are given tests from time to time. Some of them are expected as part of the curriculum and others are "surprise" tests. Whether anticipated or unanticipated, there are two ways to take a test — resist and fight or accept and grow through the experience. It's easy to be tested when everything is going well. It's when the testing is least expected that one is tempted to complain and to struggle. The test remains a test, though, whether accepted or battled, and the requirement is still a lesson to be learned. If failed, the test must be taken again and again until the lesson is learned and you, finally, get it right.

Accept and **embrace** the test as an opportunity to grow. This produces a better attitude which will help with the outcome. In this manner, the solution is sought and earned actively rather than fought or resisted. When you are tested, determine what you can gain from the lesson life is teaching you and then learn it! It's so practical; you won't have to face it again if you get it right this time. By learning to deal with smaller issues — such as criticism from others — you will learn to handle larger trials when they come along.

Use What You Already Have

The key to the door of success is to start **NOW.** Utilize what you already have and build from there. Every "master" was once an apprentice; every professor, once a student; every doctor, an intern. You have to climb the ladder in your field, whatever that field might be. Taking a shortcut in the process often leads to difficulty or, even, disaster. You cannot wait until you are a "master" to begin, for you will never become a "master" without climbing the ladder of experience.

Excellent ways to perfect your style are to hear other speakers, read other authors, and attend other workshops. The reason is, NOT to copy their material, but to learn from what they do. The best speakers will inspire you to greatness; the poor ones will try to tell you that only they have the answers. The great ones will excite you to action; the terrible ones will bore you into a near-death experience. You will learn what audiences like, and you surely will see what flops. Practice what works, avoid what doesn't. Take time to connect with the various presenters, for such connections can help you in your own area. Offer to be of help to them — because all activity is rewarded. What you do to help others, in generosity, will come back to you multiplied many times over.

Keep your work in focus. Even though you have taken classes in various disciplines and have many interests, please stay focused on your main area of expertise. Do not become a "Jack-of-all-trades and master of none."

Although I have encouraged and, hopefully, inspired you to write more, to speak more easily, and to give programs, I also wish to encourage you to simplify your life. Perhaps that might seem a paradox, but you CAN build your life in some ways and simplify it in others. The secret is to do what *you* really want with your life. Many people tend to do what others want or expect them to do. Often, such expectations lead to conscious or subconscious resentment. You should be entitled to live your life fully — to help others and to reap the rewards of your work.

If you have distractions in life, find ways to eliminate them or at least lessen those demands. If you want to build your life in a more positive way, then to do so. Make the positive happen and lessen the difficulties. There is no magic formula that works for everyone, but there are real ways that work for real people. Decide what is productive for you and do it. Study your life to detect what is draining and then plug the leak! Down-size the status symbols and eliminate the clutter of your environment.

A Few Gifts

Throughout this book, I have striven to share valuable information gleaned mostly from my twenty years of doing similar work. I sincerely hope that my information and encouragement will be an inspiration to ACTION. Purposefully, I have kept my personal values out of the book and have kept it to the point as much as possible. Keep in mind that I do not want any "followers" because I believe that people should follow **their own** higher guidance and inner wisdom. I will be quite contented just to make it through this lifetime without offending myself or anyone else too much. I have no easy answers to life's dilemmas nor magic pills for society's ills. Somehow, though, I would feel amiss if I did not include a final gift, some parting wisdom from my years of spiritual research and discovery. Here are my final gifts for you — not from theory, but from years of practical work.

1.   Whatever you do in your life — good or bad — will return to you eventually. It is termed, "what you plant, you will reap" or otherwise stated, "what you are now reaping, you once planted," even though you might have forgotten what you planted, where or when.

2.   Be generous. That generosity will come back to you. Don't look for the reward; it will come in its own time when the harvest is ripe and full.

3. Find ways to be of service to humanity — not only by contributing a few dollars to a favorite cause, but in daily interaction with others. Seek ways to serve

with passion and compassion for all. Some people might cheat you and might take advantage of you occasionally; but you will learn and will gain the more for it. Service to others will bring your greatest purpose and achievement.

4.   Live your heart's passion. Do whatever it is that excites your inner light and passion. Live exuberantly with purpose and excitement. TRULY MAKE YOUR DAILY LIFE AN ADVENTURE.

5.   Dare to be you! It has been said often that only the great minds dare to be different. Conversely, perhaps it is that very daring and courage — or that difference — that makes one great. Take the initiative, be self-reliant. Be committed to continuous learning and growing.

6.   Take time to party. Life has enough work and serious stuff — relax and have fun. After all, what is the purpose of life? To do a good job? Yes, but to enjoy it also. The fun is in the doing! DO it! Laugh, be silly, be happy!

7.   Strive to face your demanding little demons, and you'll diminish them; confront your most frightening fears, and they will begin to fade. **Boldly walk into tomorrow with a purpose and a vision for a better world.**

Chapter Nine
Building the Mind

A Tool Will Help You Only if You Use It Properly

This book is about developing and refining your communication skills. It teaches you to use your conscious and subconscious mind. The subconscious work is as valuable as the conscious work, perhaps even more so. This is the greatest gift that I can give to you — this is how you will excel. Self-hypnosis is the tool for success. All you need to do is to use it wisely.

It was approximately 35 years ago that I began experimenting with self-hypnosis. At that time, I was not sure how effective or valuable this tool would be for me. I honestly wondered if it would work. The early sessions brought no profound experience and no giant breakthrough. In fact, it was several months later before I began noticing **any** changes in my life. This probably is similar to the experience of some parents who hardly notice the daily growth of a child. Although the daily changes are not noticeable, in time, the infant grows to become an adult. Growth is usually a gradual process; betterment comes in its own way and at its own pace.

If you are unwilling to try self-hypnosis, no one can make you do it. If you **are** willing to try working with it, you **will** gain a great deal. After 35 years, I can say, emphatically, that self-hypnosis **really does work.**

Granted, as in my case, during the first few weeks or months, it might seem as if little is happening. Soon, however, the changes become clear. A better life is being built.

Self-hypnosis works because it uses your **full** brain — not fragmented parts. I have found it to be a tool that can improve the life of every person on earth. It is not a magic pill; it's a tool that is used to build and to focus the mind. A hammer is a tool that is designed to hammer nails, but it can be used for other purposes as well, or not used at all. Just as a hammer will not get up on its own initiative and start hammering, self-hypnosis will not make a person change or accomplish anything unless that person has a desire to take constructive action. The tool is just a tool — it is one's decision and free will whether or not to use it.

If this is your first time working with self-help or self-hypnosis programs, it would be a good idea to read about the field. Self-hypnosis is a safe, 100% natural and direct way to improve your life. My book, *Self-Hypnosis — Creating Your Own Destiny*, would help you to gain a deeper knowledge of the science and art of hypnosis.

The art of self-hypnosis concerns timing, tone, and delivery — not going too fast or too slow, not being too forceful nor too meek. The inner mind (subconscious) responds very differently from the conscious mind. It contains profound depth and wisdom; yet, it works slowly and requires clear, direct questions or instructions. It has a natural simplicity and honesty, and is uncomplicated in its approach.

Creating Your Own Destiny encourages people to make their own self-hypnosis tapes by reading scripts aloud into their cassette recorder. Some people say they don't like the sound of their own voices on cassette tape.

Paradoxically, this very apparatus that they don't like is the very tool that will help them.

Work with your cassette recorder, in the privacy of your room, and practice speaking differently. Yes deliberately, you can change the physical sound of your own voice, bring to it a tone and delivery that pleases you. If you have a high pitch, speak lower or deeper. If you mumble, begin to speak distinctly. If you normally speak in a monotone, add life and enthusiasm to your voice. Do whatever is necessary to improve the pitch, modulation, and speed of your voice. In just an hour, or even less, you will have improved the quality of your voice.

An ironic aspect of self-hypnosis is that you TRUST your own voice more than other voices. As you learn to improve your voice, you also will learn about self-hypnosis — in the doing. Theory is fine, but there is no substitute for practical experience.

Are you ready now to make your own self-help, self-hypnosis tape? Get a cassette recorder with a good microphone and a blank tape. To record, find a place where you will not be distracted for about an hour. First, read the following script aloud and make any changes, deletions, or additions which suit your personal preferences. Now, read the script slowly into your cassette tape. Speak s-l-o-w-l-y, very slowly, less than half your normal pace; even slower is better. Use your watch and time the one-minute pauses for one FULL minute. The subconscious mind needs that much time to process the question and to give you the information requested.

In time, when you become more proficient at making self-hypnosis tapes, you can add the sound of a grandfather clock ticking in the background, or the soothing music of one of the Old Masters, or the gentle sounds of the New Age genre.

Constructive Imagination

Each script includes exercises for using your imagination. Imagination is like a door to your inner mind. The constructive imagination can help build a better reality. It is similar to **pretending.**

Many people assume that pretending is something phony or undesirable. In truth, pretending is a valuable process of creation, in spite of the implication of children's pretending or the hint that it is unsophisticated to pretend. Words like constructive imagination, positive thinking, visualization, and faith are used as substitute words.

The inner or subconscious mind is quite different from the conscious mind. It perceives pretending as a valid part of eventual accomplishment. Research on how the mind works suggests that when we pretend that something will happen, it has a far better chance of happening than when we don't. This works in both positive and negative pretending. Going a step further produces even more dramatic results. When we pretend or imagine that something is *already accomplished,* the inner mind perceives it as accomplished. Use this valuable discovery to help you in your self-hypnosis sessions. **Pretend** that you already are a good writer, a dynamic speaker, an excellent presenter. In so doing, you will become exceptional!

Once your tape is completed, find quiet times to enjoy using your tape. Making tapes is easy — using them is a pleasure. Self-hypnosis relaxes the body, builds the mind, and energizes your life in amazing and wonderful ways. It is a "win-win-win" activity with great benefit to be gained and no down-side. Remember to breathe deeply throughout the session, for deep breathing is one of the oldest and most effective methods of relaxation.

Artist: Kathye Mendes

When we pretend or imagine that something is already accomplished, the inner mind perceives it as accomplished.

Use your tape once a day. Keep a journal or diary, and log-in the results. Describe whatever you receive: What did you see? What did you feel? What did you hear? What did you perceive? For some people, the information is fleeting, as in a dream. For others, it comes clear and strong. There is no right or wrong method for receiving and processing information. The way **you** receive information is correct for you. Your work will improve over time with experience and patience.

Use your tape for yourself or share it with friends and family. (Better still, teach them to make their own tapes!) Should a recorder not be available, read the script aloud to loved ones. If you, or they, do not like the word **hypnosis,** then you may substitute any other appropriate words that you prefer. Some terms are guided reverie, an inspired meditation, a working dream, or focusing attention.

For now, let's term the session an **inner adventure** which allows you, or others, to experience it without pre-conceptions or pre-conditions. It is simply — and profoundly — an exciting journey inward. You can experience as much (or as little) of the adventure as YOU wish.

Be gentle with yourself. Be kind to your mind! Whatever you receive or accomplish in your session is a gift from your subconscious mind. If you accept and welcome that gift then, surely, more will be given at another time. If you criticize your inner mind and negate or belittle your gift, then you limit your potential.

There is no best time, in a general sense, to use self-hypnosis tapes. Timing is very individual. The best time for you is at the high-point of your day. Pay attention to your daily rhythms or biological clock. They are much like tides, which ebb and flow. If you reach your peak

— or high tide — at around 10:00 a.m., then that would be the best time for you. This time might not be practical if, for instance, you must be at work at that hour. In that case, you will need to determine another time when you can profit best from your tapes. They may be used as often as you like. Once or twice a day is adequate for most people.

In self-hypnosis, we focus the conscious mind and use it as a tool to instruct and to guide the unconscious in the direction that we consciously want our lives to go. Self-hypnosis can be symbolized by a microscope focusing on a specific goal or objective.

Your mind is your most valuable resource. By using self-help tapes, you train your mind to use more of its vast potential. You extend the boundaries of your reality.

Pessimists blame others for their lack of success in life, or they blame circumstances. Optimists hope that everything will work out without any effort on their behalf — that others will do it all for them. But, **realists** take responsibility for their lives and make their own self-hypnosis tapes for the success and betterment of their life experiences!

Throughout your adventure, remember that TRUST is the key to the door of your higher mind, and APPRECIATION makes the opening easier. BE THANKFUL for all that you receive, and you will gain and grow as you journey the path of life.

Artist: Sue Jones

Trust is the key to the door of your higher mind.

Building the Mind: Enhancing Creativity

This section contains three Inner Adventure scripts for self-help and self-betterment:
1. Inspired Writing
2. Public Speaking
3. Teaching and Learning

Inner Adventure #1 — *Inspired Writing*

This guided session is an Inner Adventure to help your writing. This creative technique utilizes the inner mind for guidance and inspiration. You may use the same procedures for inspired drawing as well. All people have the latent ability to communicate with their higher minds. For some, it's easier than for others, but we all can do it, and it gets easier over time.

The following eight guidelines will assist you in preparing for your Inspired Writing sessions. Make a tape using the script that follows. Use your tape as often as you wish. A journal or spiral notebook will keep your writings grouped in a neat, orderly manner. Do not read your writings immediately, but put them aside for a few days or even weeks, to give a space between your inspiration and your evaluations.

1.   Choose a regular, specific time period to do the work. Set the mood, dim the lights and have a pencil or pen and paper ready. (You could also use typewriter, computer, or word processor.)

2.   Set aside a quiet time when you can relax the body and mind. If you already work with a favorite technique, then use it to help you enter your intuitive level of relaxation. If not, then just take a few minutes to remember a time when you really felt safe and comfortable.

3. Visualize yourself in a protective field or bubble of light and love. Offer a prayer for guidance and affirm your creative goals and ideals.

4. Put aside your ego and write, type, or draw whatever comes to you. This is the fun part so don't make a big deal of it. Just do it! Write or sketch your thoughts, feelings, or impressions.

5. Take neither credit nor blame for what comes through. Don't reread it now. Just put it away for awhile and review it days or weeks from now.

6. Strive to make this communication come from within. Do not draw from outside influences. Connect with your own higher self — your creative potential. The journey is within, the pathway is trust.

7. Be patient. Allow yourself time to receive those "Gifts" from your higher mind — they will come.

8. Do not be anxious about what others say in criticism. You do not need to show your work to anyone. Disregard any self-criticism that might surface. Many people produce beautiful, inspired work but are far too critical of their own superb accomplishments.

(Start Recording your tape here. Read the following script slowly and clearly into the microphone.)

Sit back, relax, and let your mind do the work

With your eyes closed, you may perceive even more clearly. If you take a deep breath, you can feel your body relaxing. As you slow your breathing, you let your mind relax.

Begin by comparing your mind to the surface of a quiet pond. My voice can be as a breeze whispering in the trees along the shore. The pond remains smooth and calm, even though things go on beneath the surface.

There may be much happening beneath a still surface. The gentle surface conceals extraordinary depth. Reflect upon nature, its beauty and elegance.

(Pause, one minute)

Now it is easy to dissolve this image and to form another — perhaps a stairway leading down — you can see yourself leisurely descending. The stairs are covered with a thick, plush carpet, a carpet that is like a cloud beneath your feet. Perhaps there is a brass handrail or a walnut banister. The stairs lead you to a ballroom with sparkling crystal chandeliers, or to a comfortable room with books. There are crackling logs in a fireplace. And while you are here, the outside world will stay outside. You can take a few minutes and notice just how good you feel here.

(Pause, one minute)

You can do anything you want to do. You don't even have to listen to my voice, because your subconscious hears with new awareness and responds all by itself.

You are now learning to recognize the feelings that accompany inner relaxation. You may experience a light, medium, or deep level of relaxation; you choose what is best for you. Your body may feel heavy, or it may feel light, or it may seem to be asleep so that it doesn't feel anything at all. It may float up, or it may sink down, or it may very pleasantly drift. It may do whatever you wish. Perhaps your body feels as if it has gone to sleep even though your mind seems to be awake. Of course, you don't have to concern yourself with that.

This is a learning and growing experience. Of course, you may go very deep — and safely. Your inner mind is aware; it realizes when it needs to respond and can do so in just the right way. It already has gained more awareness.

If I count from ten to one, then you may go deeper — more in perfect harmony — by picturing yourself descending a flight of stairs, or going down in an elevator or on an escalator — any pleasant image that you wish... (slowly) ten, nine, eight, seven, six, five, four, three, two, one.

And if I count from ten to one again, you may go twice as deep, enjoying a pleasant, comfortable feeling — any sort of feeling that you wish... (more slowly) ten, nine, eight, seven, six, five, four, three, two, one.

As you relax, take a deep breath, and slow down. You may go even deeper. As you enjoy the comfort, you will note that there is less and less importance to my voice. You may find yourself drifting in your own ideal, joyful place of relaxation.

(Pause, one minute)

And in this place of relaxation, there is a light. A protective light which fills your entire being and extends beyond the physical body itself — filling your energy field. This is a light of protection, of strength, of wisdom, and purpose.

You can begin this exercise by asking your higher guidance to come through. Simply ask to receive your highest source of wisdom and counsel. Ask for inspiration and information that will be of benefit to you and to others.

Perhaps you will be shown visions. If so, sketch those scenes or describe them in words. Listen to your thoughts or feelings. Trust the impressions that you receive. Write those thoughts or describe those feelings on paper.

Open your eyes just wide enough to see through your peripheral vision — enough to keep pen upon paper. Keep your arm and hand light, flowing. Write whatever

comes to mind. Nobody else can do this for you; you're
the one who does it. Just begin writing or sketching...

(NOTE: Before recording your tape, decide how long
you wish your inspired writing sessions to be. At first,
ten to fifteen minutes will be adequate. Leave that
amount of time blank on your tape. Later, twenty
minutes — or more, may be your desire. Leave that
amount of time blank on your tape.)

And now, to complete the exercise, simply rest the
eyes, rest the hand, just rest a moment. Now thank your
higher mind, your inner guidance, for the information
given here today. You have done very well, and it is
time to return from your Inner Adventure.

I will count slowly from one to ten. At the count of
ten, you may open your eyes and be wide awake.

One:	Coming up slowly.
Two:	Remember what you have been given here today.
Three:	Total normalization at every level of your being.
Four:	You may wish to move hands, or feet, or neck.
Five:	Thankful for the gifts of your higher mind.
Six:	Remember to put the writings aside for a few days.
Seven:	Coming up to your full potential.
Eight:	Revitalized.
Nine:	Re-energized.
Ten:	Open your eyes and wide awake now. Wide Awake!

(Your tape is now completed and ready to use.)

Use your tape as often as you wish. Inspired Writing is not difficult. In fact, many people use similar techniques and procedures every day. You will get from this exercise exactly what you put into it.

Inner Adventure #2 — *Public Speaking*

If you ever have stood before a group or performed in a school play, you are familiar with the uneasy feeling that occurs at such times. Almost everyone has experienced "butterflies" before. "Butterflies" quite accurately describes the feeling that occurs when adrenalin is triggered and pumped through your body to deal with a stress situation.

This program has helped bashful and reticent people to become excellent public speakers. It can help you to become a confident, effective speaker — perhaps even a verbal dynamo. Whenever you are given an opportunity to speak, use this session a few days before the scheduled event to reinforce success.

Positive suggestion and guided imagery are two of the most valuable tools in the workshop of the mind. Creative visualization adds a new dimension to thinking by using the mind's eye to picture positive actions and positive results; you can point it in the direction in which you want your life to go.

Guided by your ideals, set public speaking goals that are both realistic and attainable. Plant the seeds and nourish your mind with a vision of the reality of your goals accomplished. Picturing a positive end result can be the most exciting and fulfilling part of your session.

(Start recording your tape here.)

Breathe deeply and smoothly for a few minutes. (Pause)

You can keep your eyes open for a minute. You can look either forward or upward. I am going to count down from ten to one, and with every descending number just slowly blink your eyes. Slowly close and then open your eyes, as in slow motion, with every number... ten... nine... eight... seven... six... five... four... three... two... and one. Now you can just close your eyes, and you can keep them closed. I will explain what that was for, and why you did that.

That exercise was just to relax your eyelids. And, right now in your eyelids, there is probably a feeling of relaxation, perhaps a comfortable, tired feeling, or a pleasant, heavy sensation. Whatever feeling is right now in your eyelids, just allow that feeling to multiply, to magnify, and to become greater. Allow your eyelids to become totally and pleasantly relaxed. This is something you do; nobody else can do it for you. You are the one who does it.

Just take your time and completely and pleasantly relax your eyelids. And, as you relax your eyelids, you can allow that feeling of relaxation that is now in your eyelids to flow outward in all directions, as in imaginary waves or ripples. Allow a feeling of relaxation to go outward to the entire facial area. Just relax the head. Enjoy the relaxation as it goes to the neck and to the shoulders, down the arms and into the hands. Welcome a wonderful feeling of relaxation going down the entire body to the legs and feet, all the way out to the toes; completely and pleasantly relaxing the entire body. And you slow down a little bit. Allow yourself to slow down just a little bit. Later, as we go along, you can slow down just a little bit more.

(Pause)

There might be some movement in your eyelids. That is called rapid eye movement and is a perfectly normal and natural part of this experience. It will pass very quickly. And, in a moment, I am going to count downward once again from ten to one. This time, as you hear every descending number, just feel yourself slow down a little bit more with every number. At the number one, you can enter your own natural level of relaxation. I will count rapidly now: Ten, nine, eight, seven, six, five, four, three, two, one.

You are now at your own natural level of relaxation. From this level, you may move to any other level with full awareness and you can function at will. You are completely aware at every level of your mind even though your body may feel asleep. You can accept or reject anything which is given to you. You are in complete control. At this level, or at any other level, you can give yourself positive mental suggestions — suggestions that your inner mind can accept and act upon in a positive manner — suggestions that are designed for your success — to achieve your goals and ideals.

See yourself relaxed in mind and in body. This is something that you want; it is here and it is now. As you take a deep breath, you can enter a deeper and healthier level of mind — more in perfect harmony, more centered and balanced — with every breath you take — as the following words echo deeply with your mind:

I can be anything I want to be.
I can really understand how to feel good talking to other people.

I am becoming an effective speaker.
Emotion is a good thing;
it is an element of being human.
I enjoy that element, but emotion is less enjoyable if it
prevents me from expressing myself openly in a clear,
logical way.
If there have been times in the past
when, through emotional stress, I may have been
unable to communicate easily,
I realize this was all in the past.

Now that I am becoming an effective speaker,
I understand that the inner feelings
which I may have experienced are simply adrenalin —
my body's own abundant, natural energy,
available for me to harness and to control
at the right time
to accomplish any goal I set for myself.
Controlled adrenalin can keep me sharp and aware;
I can direct and channel it into enthusiasm and vitality.
I can become whatever I want to become,
and, with this realization,
I am becoming a successful public speaker.
I allow my own innate sensing mechanism
to let me do the right thing at the right time,
to let me say the right thing at the right time.

I speak clearly, precisely, calmly, and effectively
in a way that people can enjoy and easily relate to.
In my mind I can visualize myself
standing in front of an audience,
preparing to speak.
I take a deep breath
and feel myself continuing to breathe easily.
Smiling, I take a moment to look at the group of people.

(Pause one full minute)

My thoughts are coming into focus,
they are distinct and well-organized,
because I am cognizant of what I am going to say
to get my point across.

I am an effective speaker;
I am sure of myself
because I have prepared my material and am familiar
with it.
I see myself as calm
and vividly focus on this positive, assured image in
my mind.

(Pause one full minute)

I am an experienced speaker, expressing myself
delightfully in every situation.
This is an enjoyable and exciting experience
because I concentrate on what I am giving to the group.
I clearly deliver each important point to my audience.
I am simple, yet direct.
As I am speaking to the people,
I am loving them and serving them —
giving my gifts —
aware of what I am sharing,
helping them to learn and to grow.
Expressing the full and profound
magnetism of my soul.
I feel this as having already been accomplished.
I am thanking the audience for this opportunity to share
and to be with them.

(Pause one full minute)

I now picture myself after the talk.
Smiling people are coming up and thanking me,
saying how much they enjoyed and learned from the talk.
As they are shaking my hand,
I realize that I truly did well.
I did do a good job and am thankful for the experience
of helping others and speaking with them. (Pause)

Although your conscious mind might not remember all that you accomplished here today, your subconscious mind always remembers. It is already acting upon those suggestions and those visualized images in a positive manner. Benefit — success — can come at any time. It can come back with you now, or you can experience it in due time. And, in a little while, when you return, you will feel just wonderful. But before you come back here, be aware that you can drift back clear-headed — that you will be wide awake, refreshed, and happy.

I will count from one to ten, at the count of ten you will open your eyes, be alert, energized, and feeling fine — feeling better than before. I will count now: one... two... coming out slowly... three... four... coming up now... five... six... feel the circulation returning and equalizing... seven... eight... awakening your full potential with perfect equilibrium and normalization throughout your being... nine... ten. Open your eyes... wide awake and feeling great.

(Your tape is now completed and ready to use.)

Inner Adventure #3 — *Teaching and Learning*

Any reader skimming through this book might wonder why this section is entitled, "Teaching and Learning" — for that seems inverted. As a careful reader, you will realize that teaching and learning are intertwined, like threads in the same fabric. Who can separate teaching from learning? By teaching comes our best learning, and often we are our own best teacher and student at the same time.

We learn...
>   10% of what we read
>   20% of what we hear
>   30% of what we see
>   50% of what we both see and hear
>   70% of what is discussed with others
>   80% of what we experience personally
>   95% of what we TEACH to someone else
>   — William Glasser

Wise learning comes by using this script to make a tape that will help you to become a better teacher. And in teaching others what you have learned, you will learn even more! The very activity of teaching is creative and exciting. Don't wait for another day! Start today, by making a positive programming tape using this script. USE your tape, about once a day, and in one month you'll be amazed at the results.

(Start recording your tape now)

To begin your Inner Adventure,
get comfortable.
If you have a favorite method for entering
your natural level of relaxation,
just close your eyes, and use that method now.
Otherwise, just **breathe** deeply and smoothly
and remember a time
when you were completely relaxed and at ease,
And I will be quiet.

(Pause one full minute)

Remember to breathe deeply throughout this exercise.
With your eyes closed, perhaps you can perceive
even better.
and it becomes easier and easier
to become more and more aware
of a number of things
that often would go overlooked,
or even unnoticed.
Thoughts
Feelings
Impressions
Sensations.
As you take another deep breath and exhale...
the mind experiences
a gradual letting go.
Going to a place of relaxation
your ideal, joyful place of relaxation
where even the effort
to be aware of my voice
or the meaning of my words
almost seems too much work
to bother trying.

It is so much easier simply to allow
your conscious mind to rest
while your unconscious mind —
that quiet inner mind —
can continue to hear
and to respond to things easily
automatically.
As the conscious mind begins to drift off…
the **inner** mind allows you
to alter your experience
and to continue to learn.
Learning the FEELING of letting go
allowing the inner mind to assume
more responsibility
for guiding you
assisting you
as you wish to explore
your own abilities
and capabilities.

Perhaps your conscious mind
has already begun to drift —
to let go for a time —
while the body relaxes, the mind is
day-dreaming or in reverie.
Of course the inner mind is always aware
and continues to hear
everything of importance.

At this natural level of relaxation
you can discover
how to drift…
safely,
effortlessly.

To utilize your inner mind
to accomplish many things —
new things about old times
and old things in new ways.
Skills are like buried treasures
stored deep in the mind
waiting to be re-discovered.

You can remember what you learn
about how you allow your mind
to teach you
and guide you
in better ways
and wiser ways
of doing things.
Life becomes a journey
through time —
delighting the spirit
fascinating the mind
discovering inner realities
new talents and abilities.

Every journey is an adventure of discovery
because what you'll find is always interesting
always helpful.
In helping others, **you** are helped
In giving, **you** receive
In teaching, you also are learning.

Teaching is giving, receiving, and sharing
You are both a teacher and a learner
eager to grow, to share,
to experience.

You already are an excellent
teacher and learner
in numerous ways
you guide and help others
you share knowledge and experiences.

Now allow a memory to return
of a time when you showed somebody
how to do something.
Anything.
When you **really** enjoyed teaching someone
anyone, even a small group.
People teach in many ways.
Recall the memory vividly, clearly
and I will be quiet.

(Pause one full minute)

Hold this memory close
and now envision or imagine
a new impression.
Create a positive picture
of **future** success —
remembering your future.

Bring into this scene
some of your writings
your research,
listen to your talks
Add the charisma of your personality.
Bring this all together
and wrap it into a beautiful package
a gift of your future
and I will be quiet.

(Pause one full minute)

Make this vision real and alive
Place yourself prominently in the picture.
Make yourself "star" of the show.
And imagine that it is already accomplished,
that you already are
a creative writer
a successful speaker
a powerful presenter
A self-directed learner.

(Pause one full minute)

Writing, speaking, teaching, learning,
open your highest levels
of inspiration and genius.
In application and activity
you raise your level of expertise
and produce valuable materials.

(Pause one full minute)

At both the inner and outer levels
you are building "people" skills.
You like people and they like you.
You genuinely like others
and they sincerely like you.
You respect people and they respect you.
You help others and they help you.

Listen carefully now as I whisper
a great truth... (whisper)
Success is both the journey

and the destination… (end whisper)
The more successful you are
the more you refine,
develop, and utilize
your creative skills.
You live life fully
and thankfully
with passion and compassion.
You work diligently
and excel in many skills.
You communicate easily with others
in ways they understand
simply
honestly
with warmth and humor.
You love learning.
You love teaching small groups
as easily
as presenting to large audiences.
You are a "natural" —
Naturally!

And now,
before you allow yourself to come up completely
to your conscious level
it may be wise
to utilize
the opportunity to assimilate
all that you have experienced.
For, in the future, you will discover
new insights
a sudden understanding or revelation
you haven't thought of before.
It will be your inner mind

giving to your conscious mind
things that you **already** knew,
but didn't realize that you knew.
Because we all do our own learning
in our own time,
in our own way,
with a sense of purpose.

And now, take all the time that you wish;
time can appear longer than it actually is
or shorter...
Take your time
and begin coming back,
coming up to your everyday reality. (Pause)

Tell yourself it's time to come up now
Wide awake, refreshed,
feeling better than before
Open your eyes, and wide awake.

(Your tape is completed and ready to use.)

Note: use your journal to record all impressions, feelings, or insights gained from this and other inner adventures. Write, in detail, the pre-views of your future success.

Appendix
Resources

Resources

Throughout two decades of writing, speaking, and teaching workshops, I have called upon many sources for aid and assistance. In this book, I have shared with you the very best of what I have learned — much of which came through trial and error. If I can be of further help or encouragement in this field, please write to me with your **specific questions**, and I will respond.

The list on the following pages is not a comprehensive one, but it does contain some of my best resources and their names and addresses.

I was not compensated in any way for recommending the individuals or businesses. This is simply a free bonus for you, the reader. I believe that when credit is due, it should be given. While it is impossible to list here my many helpers and my sources for materials, I have noted my primary resources. The individuals and companies may be contacted directly.

Writing:

Most of the people who help me with writing and editing do so freely and as friends. One lady does offer her services professionally, and at a very reasonable fee;
Linda Hutchins
c/o Adventures Into Time Publishers
P.O. Box 88
Independence, VA 24348

Printing:

I believe it is best to have your printing done locally, so that you can follow through in person. Some printers perform adequately through the mails, but local printers have served me very well for many years. My favorite local printers:
Wordsprint, Inc.
P.O. Box 544
Wytheville, VA 24382

Logo Design, Graphic Art, Illustration, Desktop Publishing:

Sue Jones
P.O. Box 140464
Grand Rapids, MI 49514

Brochure Design and Layout:

Veronica Reed
503 Lake Drive
Virginia Beach, VA 23451

Deborah Greer
P.O. Box 648
Independence, VA 24348

Book Manufacturer:

I have dealt with a few publishers and book
manufacturers. BookCrafters is the best I have found.
They can provide valuable suggestions for your project.
Write for a free estimate on your book.
BookCrafters
Jeanne Atkinson
P.O. Box 370
Chelsea, MI 48118

Book Distribution:

New Leaf Distribution Co.
401 Thornton Rd.
Lithia Springs, GA 30057

Two Publishers:

Dan Poynter guides publishers in promoting their
books. Write for a free copy of "Publishing Poynters".
Para Publishing
P.O. Box 8206-271
Santa Barbara, CA 93118-8206

Dick Sutphen has written several best-selling books
on metaphysics, published numerous other books, and
produced many audio and video tapes. His pioneering

work has helped and has inspired millions of people around the world. Write for free information.

Valley of the Sun Publishing
P.O. Box 38
Malibu, CA 90265

Public Speaking:

Toastmasters International
P.O. Box 9052
Mission Viejo, CA 92690

My Three Favorite International Organizations:

The Edgar Cayce organization is headquartered at Virginia Beach, Virginia. Members and study groups abound in virtually every country in the world. This is a large, dedicated organization of spiritual seekers. I have been a member for over 33 years, and I suggest that you write to them for free information — you'll be glad that you did!

The Association for Research and Enlightenment
Box 595
Virginia Beach, VA 23451

I am a member of various hypnosis and healing organizations. The National Guild of Hypnotists is among the very best by far. Membership is all-inclusive and offers a forum for the discussion and practical use of hypnosis.

In August of every year, the National Guild sponsors a large convention, inviting hundreds of speakers. This is the best in the world! Write for free information. I highly recommend them.

The National Guild of Hypnotists
Box 308
Merrimack, NH 03054

My third favorite organization consists, primarily, of therapists, serious students, and researchers, but membership is open to the public. APRT offers a major conference each spring and autumn, as well as the presentation of study group programs across the country throughout the year. This is a smaller organization, but it does amazing work — and on a large scale. Write for more information.

Association for Past-Life Research and Therapies
Box 20151
Riverside, CA 92516

Books, Tapes & Video by Henry Leo Bolduc

Simply Check the items you want:

❑ **Self-Hypnosis: Creating Your Own Destiny**
In three easy steps you can create your own self-help tapes. There is no limit to what you can do! 10th printing. Quality paperback, 190 pages, $9.95

❑ **The Journey Within**
Past-life regression and channeling. A fascinating journey into our deepest memories. Quality paperback, 299 pages, $12.95

❑ **Life Patterns, Soul Lessons and Forgiveness**
Ever feel that you're repeating the same patterns in your life? Those patterns could have roots which extend far into the past, deep into the psyche. Quality paperback, 300 pages, illustrated, $14.95

❑ **Your Creative Voice**
Learn how to reach out through writing and speaking. This hands-on, how-to book gives practical information on conducting workshops. Whether you want a career in workshop presentation or just want to speak occasionally, this book is sure to help. Quality paperback, 208 pages, illustrated, $14.95

❑ **Life Patterns — The Video**
Highlights from the Life Patterns workshop. Video cassette, $24.95

❏ **Healing the Past — Building the Future**
Side 1: "Discovering the Healer Within." Everyone has healing potential and healing gifts.
Side 2: "Your Extraordinary Journey Through Time" is our newest session for age-regression, past-life exploration, and future progression. Progression is the history of your future!
Audio cassette tape, $9.98

❏ **Embracing Your Eternal Child**
Side 1: "Embracing Your Eternal Child" helps you connect with that innocent and wonderful child within, to experience the incredible healing power of love.
Side 2: "Inspired Writing or Drawing." Write messages from your Healer-in-Residence, your Financial Advisor, your Inner Jester, and your Higher Self.
Audio cassette tape, $9.98

❏ **Pack Your Bags**
Side 1: "A Journey Through Time." Embark upon a journey of self-discovery and self-enlightenment.
Side 2: "The Treasures of Your Past", to touch and to recover the tangible treasures hidden in your memory.
Audio cassette tape, $9.98

Order Form

Qty	Title	Price Ea	Total
	Self-Hypnosis	9.95	
	The Journey Within	12.95	
	Life Patterns — Book	14.95	
	Your Creative Voice	14.95	
	Life Patterns — Video	24.95	
	Healing the Past	9.98	
	Eternal Child	9.98	
	Pack Your Bags	9.98	

SubTotal	
VA Residents add 4.5% Sales Tax	
Shipping and Handling	**$1.75**
TOTAL	

PLEASE PRINT YOUR NAME & ADDRESS

Name _____

Address _____

City, State, Zip _____

Mail to: **Adventures Into Time**
P.O. Box 88
Independence, VA 24348

Payment by check or money order, payable to: **Adventures Into Time.** Please, no phone orders. Money back guarantee if not satisfied — within 90 days of purchase.

Photocopy order form if you want extra copies.